Discoveries
for
Peaceful
Living

Discoveries for Peaceful Living

DAVID A. RAY

Fleming H. Revell Company
Old Tappan, New Jersey

Scripture quotations identified as KJV are from the *King James Version of the Bible.*

Scripture quotations identified as RSV are from the *Revised Standard Version of the Bible,* Copyrighted 1946 and 1952.

Scripture quotations identified as TEV are from the *Today's English Version of the New Testament.* Copyright © American Bible Society 1966.

Scripture quotations identified as NEB are from *The New English Bible, New Testament.* © The Delegates of the Oxford University Press and the Syndics of the Cambridge University Press 1961. Reprinted by permission.

Scripture quotations identified as LB are from *The Living Bible.* Copyright © 1971 by Tyndale House Publishers, Wheaton, Illinois. All rights reserved.

Scripture quotations identified as PHILLIPS are from *The New Testament in Modern English* translated by J. B. Phillips, copyright J. B. Phillips, 1958. Used by permission of the Macmillan Company.

Scripture quotations identified as MOFFATT are from *The Bible: A New Translation* by James Moffatt. Copyright, 1954, by James Moffatt. By permission of Harper & Row, Publishers, Inc.

"The Hollow Men" by T. S. Eliot is from *Collected Poems 1909–1962,* and is used by permission of the publisher, Harcourt Brace Jovanovich, Inc.

The selection "Don't Seek to Live" is from *Prayers* by Michel Quoist, © Sheed and Ward Inc., 1963. Used by permission.

Material in this volume which appeared in *Peace Through A New You!* Copyright © 1971 by David A. Ray is used by permission of the author.

ISBN   0   8007   0513   0
Copyright © 1972 David A. Ray
All Rights Reserved
Library of Congress Catalog Card Number: 70-184572
Printed in the United States of America

To the staff of Valley Community Drive-In Church and Inspirational Living—my associates whose confidence, trust, and assistance deeply motivate me to minister in every way possible—I affectionately dedicate this book.

To my wonderful and understanding congregation in San Dimas, California, who allowed me time to write this book.

To my secretarial staff—especially Carolyn Andringa—without whom this manuscript would still be a collection of scribbled pages.

To my lovely wife, Pat, the most enthusiastic helper and supporter I have, whose encouragement gave me the courage to attempt this book.

Contents

Introduction   9

Success is for real people . . . in a real world!   11

There's enough to meet every need!   27

I can win over worry – in this life   45

Tranquility without tranquilizers and tantrums   61

Live confidently and free from tension. . . . Yes, me!   75

Marriage can really be beautiful!   89

Release the power to reach the stars   105

My misfortune can be fortunate   117

A supply of amazing optimism   129

Joy can be mine – always!   143

Introduction

At age thirty-four, life was a reasonably comfortable cruise. I had been a Christian since my teen years. Besides, I was a minister (somebody supposed to have a definite hold on life!). I pastored a young, fast-growing congregation. Already a book of mine had been published by a prestigious company. A new television ministry with high promise was underway. I was considered an optimist and a persistent doer.

I had never been one to claim that life is always easy. Accustomed to tough challenges, I seemed to move forward in quest of whatever goal to which I had set my mind.

Then something happened.

It was a six-month night!

During that time, I felt that I, as a person and human being, was in dissolution.

Depression, discouragement, tension, lostness, confusion, emptiness, and nothingness brought on unbearably long and sleepless nights. They seemed to grow on me. Days became dull and eventually dripped with gloom. Hope looked like a thing of the past.

I felt nothing of God, yet, the thread of faith still lingering within would not let me forget that a Christian isn't trouble-free; that feeling doesn't determine the involvement of God in one's life; that faith accepted and applied — in one's heart and life — produces capability and cope-ability with or without good feelings.

Never did I dream that the tears of my soul would bring about *Discoveries for Peaceful Living*. A crisis may be a cross to or a crucible of great experiences and ideas. I am grateful that the crisis has become a crucible of ideas for me. These discoveries have led me to new dimensions in living. They have deepened my life more than I ever imagined; they have given me a more realistic empathy with people — their true struggles, problems, heartaches, feelings, and possibilities; they have enriched my thinking far beyond the level prior to that experience.

I feel like the men mentioned in Matthew 20:34. Once they were blind, then "Jesus . . . touched their eyes . . . they could see, and followed him" (LB).

Another outcome of these discoveries is the peaceful Spirit growing in me. More than ever, three assurances are etching their way into my daily experience.

Thou [God] wilt keep him in perfect peace, whose mind is stayed on thee: because he trusteth in thee. Isaiah 26:3, KJV.

I am leaving you with a gift — peace of mind and heart! . . . So don't be troubled or afraid. John 14:27, LB.

. . . experience God's peace, which is far more wonderful than the human mind can understand. His peace will keep your thoughts and your hearts quiet and at rest as you trust in Christ Jesus. Philippians 4:7, LB.

The thoughts in this book reflect deeper discoveries of my own, although I know they are not original with me. These thoughts do not represent a theological dissertation; they are from a heart to the heart. They are written for people as they are. They are a personal sharing — one human being in the act of becoming more Christian to human beings in a real, tough world.

I pray that you will become a Discoverer and make some discoveries for yourself.

DAVID A. RAY

FIRST DISCOVERY

Success is for real people . . . in a real world!

Success (the real thing) is like sitting behind the wheel of a new car. There's power to it.

Success is like getting into a newly washed automobile. There's a clean smell to it — an aroma, a fresh scent.

Success is like the first sip of hot coffee on a cold morning. There's a warmth to it as it slides down your throat.

Success is like a swallow of ice cold tea with a dash of lemon on a wilting afternoon. There's a tingle to it.

Success is like putting on a new suit. You feel more like meeting people.

Success is like slipping into soft house shoes after a long, hard, tedious, tiring day. It's relaxing.

But is success something that always happens to the *other* person? You yearn wistfully, "Why can't it happen to me?"

Stop this moment! It can happen to *you!*

Yes, *you!*

You aren't designated to be a *success spectator!*

You have full possibilities of becoming a *success somebody!*

Some people feel that the stars control them and nothing can be done about it. Fate guides their lives. Even worse, some claim that God has pegged them as success spectators, at best!

But ". . . God wants his children to live in peace and harmony" (I Corinthians 7:15, LB) and ". . . to be free from worry" (7:32).

Jesus clarified it when He said, "If you live your life in me, and my words live in your hearts, you can ask for whatever you like and it will come true for you. This is how my Father will be glorified [honored]—in your becoming fruitful and being my disciples [followers]" (John 15:7, PHILLIPS).

That is one of the clearest success declarations to be found anywhere. It is one of the greatest! You may stack all the self-image psychology books in a pile and go through them with a fine tooth comb, and you will not find a more adequate success creed than this one! Perhaps you didn't know the Bible had such words. And perhaps you never realized Jesus made such startling success promises.

Richard Llewelyn expresses the idea in his book, *How Green Was My Valley.*

"Bad thoughts and greediness, Hugh," my father said, "want all, take all, and give nothing. The world was made on a different notion. You will have everything from the ground if you will ask the right way. All things are given by God, and to God you must look for what you will have."

PRINCIPLES OF TRUE SUCCESS

I have begun to discover eight principles of true success.

Success That Really Counts

What is success? In order to know, we must pull off the masks and get to the real, wonderful stuff.

You have a drink for breakfast — maybe two. The first one doesn't seem to satisfy that growl inside, not to mention the spiritual gnawing. You half-fumble your way through getting dressed, muttering how tired you feel. You stumble out of the front door for another day on the job — possibly a high-paying job. (At least you have a job, so thank God!)

And you call *that* success!

You hang your hat in a house located on Plush Street, and make frantic efforts to keep everything up. ("Most of us can't afford to be there," one person who lives there confided in me.) You're a valuable cog in the great American debt machine — a true-blue part of the fantastic *indebted society* — like the man who was asked if he was able to live within his income. "You've got to be kidding!" he replied. "I do well to live within my credit!"

And you call *that* success!

Your life is wrapped up in *things* — at least, you are preoccupied with them. This message is one the younger generation is desperately attempting to get across to Mom and Dad.

Reared in a prosperous society, they haven't faced tough challenges. They teethed in an unsacrificial surrounding, and parents mistakenly handed things to them on a golden platter—*things*—not life! They've grown up under the influence of an uncommitted church —a church that hasn't called them to personal commitment in faith to Jesus Christ. Now they are crying out, "Away with this superficial way! Away with phony living! Show me something to sink my heart into for real living!" Whether or not we like the way they are saying it, we should be grateful for what is at the bottom of it!

A seventeen-year-old daughter wrote, "Dad asks 'What in the world do you have to gripe about? You have your own car, personal telephone, large bedroom —newly remodeled I might add—and built-in stereo. Don't forget the round-the-world trip your mother and I plan on giving you for graduation.' My whole life is things—which I'd gladly give up in exchange for an honest conversation. I've never had one with either of my parents."

Care, love, a real relationship—this girl longs for them!

Is stocking up on goodies the success that really counts? *No!*

Goodies aren't bad. (Inherently, there is nothing anti-Christian to *things;* but there is more to living than things.) Become a goodie (a really good person), but be a goodie from the inside out.

Jesus emphasized that His strength "comes from doing the will of God who sent me and finishing his work" (John 4:34, LB).

You, too—in the world of everyday life! Do what you are here to do! You have everything you need with which to do it! If it is not in hand, the heavenly Father will open the doors for you—miraculously, if need be!

Things are good if they are based on such a foundation; that's success that really counts. Discoverers have this basis for success.

Use Success Words

Words are important. The telephone company has us geared to a three-minute conversation. How much can be said in three minutes? A lot — and a lot of nothing! Slow talkers can deliver about 450 words; fast talkers can almost double that.

Lincoln used 267 words for the Gettysburg Address; Shakespeare used 363 words for Hamlet's soliloquy, "To Be or Not to Be." The Lord's Prayer contains 56 words. (Phenomenal, isn't it? The greatest and most effective prayer ever offered — and probably the briefest!) The Ten Commandments, the moral standard for mankind, uses only 297 words, yet a U.S. government order dealing with the price of cabbage totals 26,911!

Many people have failure scars because they use failure words. Surrendering to a negative appetite, they spew out a conversation that defeats them. Are *you* doing it? Then practice these interesting lines, handed me by a friend.

> I'm careful of the words to say,
> To keep them soft and sweet.
> I never know from day to day,
> Which ones I'll have to eat.
> — ANONYMOUS

Words are powerful. With them, you can scathe or scintillate; belittle or build; exalt or exhaust; fake or fill; lose or lead; limp or lift; humiliate or honor; fuss or free.

For example, what can be done from words beginning with *f?* You may use failure words like *fear* and *filth,* or success words like *faith* and *full.* With *i* and *l,* you may think of *ill* and *kill,* or *skill* and *fill.* With *n* and *o,* you may think of *no* or *on.*

Words convey your spirit. Now you know why the Bible advises you to make your language winsome and wholesome. Manner in speech needs some manners. Conversation needs conversion.

Words reflect you. We must make our yes, *yes* and our no, *no!* "Well, maybe"; "We'll see about that"; "Uh, I'm not sure"; "Perhaps, later" are wishy-washy statements. When I hear them or use them, I think of the giant ocean swells I saw while I was aboard the U.S.S. *Hornet.* They rolled backward and forward, to and fro, getting nowhere. They had motion, but no movement.

There is a successful decisiveness, deliberateness, and definiteness to yes and no. Sometimes you need time to arrive at the right decision, but, when the moment comes to employ those words, do so with enthusiasm and firmness.

Stock your vocabulary with success words. Include *win, victory,* and *now* among them. Utilize success words in becoming a successful human being.

Live Your Day

Just before a rehearsal, a bassoon player told the great Toscanini that he had dropped his instrument and could not play E-flat. Toscanini lowered his head for a few moments and looked at the sheet of music. Then he lifted it again and said, "That's all right. E-flat doesn't appear in your music today."

Another's day *is not* your day for today! Stop trying to make it so! You must live *your* day — not someone else's! Elmer Leterman, one of the outstanding salesmen of the twentieth century, calls it "having the courage of your own originality."

Have you been stepping to the tune of another's day?

> *"He's* done this — I've got to do it, too."
> "I certainly have to best *him.*"
> *"He* feels I must do this, so I must do it."

He, him, and *they* are dictating your life. You're shell-shocking yourself. Sooner or later, you will have to face the issue: "It is *my* day I must live."

A young mother came to our counseling center for help, admitting that she was at the end of her rope. We probed, in an effort to find out what "the end" meant and how she had got there.

She had been reared by an exceptionally fine family in which love was a way of life. She had done extraordinarily well in school and other activities. Anything she undertook, she finished, and many people admired her for the thoroughness that characterized her life from early childhood.

An accomplished homemaker, she didn't lack interests. She was superb in sports, and a leader in her church. Three delightful children and a hard-working husband blessed her home. Money wasn't plentiful, but they made ends meet and managed to save a little.

"I don't know," she said in bewilderment.

It didn't take long to discover that her whole life was jacked up by what *others* expected of her. She had never actually thrilled to living *her* life, through a positive identification of *her* self.

Don't seek to live
somebody else's life;
it's just not you. . . .
You have no right
to put on a false face,
to pretend you're what you're not,
Say to yourself:
I am going to bring something new
into this person's life.
because he has never met anyone like me
nor will he ever meet anyone like me,
for in the mind of God
I am unique and irreplaceable.

MICHEL QUOIST

Live your own day. This is what your God wishes.
This is what your God offers. This is what your God
makes available.

Pay the Price

Success *free?* Who's kidding whom?

Often, when I speak at religious gatherings, I say,
"When you commit your life to Jesus Christ, it will cost
you *your* life. God takes it, then gives it back to you
bigger and better than ever."

One woman in California told us how much she liked
to eat. (Don't most of us! Taste makes waist, Americans
have discovered!) She found herself the victim of an
insatiable appetite.

"I'd eat half a cake in an afternoon," she confessed.
"Yet, I wanted to be slim and trim. I must lose these
pounds, even if it means going to a hypnotist." She
envisioned herself once again fitting into her bathing suit
which, lately, she had been unable to squeeze, squirm,
jiggle, or blast into.

Then a friend loaned her *God Is Fabulous* by Frances Gardner. It helped her realize that she needed to pay the price. She relinquished her appetite to God.

"It is in Your hands, Lord," she said.

Did she gain weight? Lose some? Remain the same? The essential fact was: *She became willing to pay the price!* No longer did she have to fight a raging appetite. The desire was displaced by a calm, cool, spiritual control.

"Really, I got to the point where I didn't want all that food," she smiled. And she shed those excess pounds, which is exactly what she wanted to do all along — *but,* she paid the price!

Some people are afraid to do that in life. They have the notion that they will come out second best. Is that true? Let's think of the woman in California again. By paying the price, she was given what she wanted in the first place, *plus* a feeling of excitement.

Paying the price does not infer there is a net cost; the price can return fantastic dividends.

Jim Kennedy has built a marvelous congregation of more than 3,000 members in Fort Lauderdale, Florida, over a span of fifteen years. During a day of declining churchianity (thank the Lord!) he has led in the upsurge of a dynamic fellowship. The price has been paid — by Jim, his staff, and dedicated laymen. But who can possibly say it has cost?

Who is the poorer? Anybody? Of course not!

So it is with success. Many people fail to succeed because their wishbone is where the *price*-bone must be. The price *must* be paid! There is no cut-rate price; no shortcut. Still, it doesn't cost! People who pay the price will have what it takes to give what it takes.

Know What You're After

Baron Lytton claims that the man who succeeds is one who clearly discerns his object and habitually directs his powers toward it.

Do you honestly know what your objective is? Many people do not; practically speaking, they wander their lives away.

Do you know what your needs are?

On the way to New York, I sat next to a despondent man who thought he had only two needs: money and a job. A casualty of aerospace engineering layoffs in Los Angeles, he had made his way back East, hoping to locate work. On the plane, he realized that he had *three* needs, and that money and a job took a back seat to the third: a peaceful outlook on life that is bigger than any individual development in a life.

This outlook turns men up on jobs, and jobs up on men. People who have it may have all the money they *need*.

What steps should you follow to find out what you are after? or *should* be after?

1) *List* your abilities and your disabilities. (Don't let disabilities shut up your life or tarnish your abilities. Put them in a supportive role by letting them point out ability areas, in which you can concentrate your energies.)
2) *Find* the biggest need you can, into which you can pour yourself and fill it—a worthwhile need, naturally.
3) *Evaluate* the abilities you have against the need you may fill. (There is always a match of abilities and energies for the need *you* should fill.)
4) *Ask* God to point out the way. (Unusual insight may open up to you.)
5) *Commence*—now, today—with what you have, where

you are, whether you have little or much. (There is fabulous power to beginning! Like a diesel engine, you will pick up more power after you have begun.)

Keep With It

Commencing is anchored by continuing.

"Having started . . . you should carry . . . through to completion" (II Corinthians 8:11, LB).

Nothing fails as completely as an on and off approach. *Success is a journey.* More than a single achievement, it must become the process from commencement to the crown of your undertakings. The granddaddy of all undertakings is life; therefore, keeping with life is the primary scheme of success.

There's a story about a young chemist who made a new soft drink formula and tried to market it under the name of One-Up. When it failed, he changed it to Two-Up, then Three-Up, and so on through Six-Up. At that point, he let discouragement take over and gave up. He never realized how close he was to success.

It's a humorous story, but also truthful!

Often, the significant difference between failure and success is time. One man gives up in despair; another man profits by his mistakes and moves on, perhaps in a different way.

Who is the champion except the one who goes one round more?

Can there be a more effective answer to a rebuff than a rebound?

When something is right and you believe you are the one to do it, keep with it!

You can always have keep-with-it power. When you feel it running out, you can tap a stream that never runs dry; take from a hand that is never empty; receive from a source that is always available. They are plugged in to a generator at work around the clock.

Use the Right Means

Using the right means is absolutely basic to success, because wrong means invariably wind up at wrong ends. Huckleberry Finn fooled no one when he made fun of doing it right, because it was troublesome to do right and no trouble to do wrong.

A young man came to talk over his life with me — frankly, it was a lack of life. "I'm hooked," he began drowsily, "on drugs."

Bert was from an upper-middle class family. Before getting gutted by dope, he had had hopes of graduating from college and going on to law school. And he could have made it, for Bert was a gifted man who had polluted his means to an end.

"When did you start on drugs?" I asked.

"Two years ago. Just a puff of pot — that's how I started."

"Why?"

"I wanted a lift. I felt down, and I wanted to be happy."

A lift is great. People may be happy. The question is: What will bring a genuine lift and happiness? Not superficial things; they are wrong means. Bert finally found out that wrong means deliver horrible results. It is troublesome to do wrong!

You can be certain that: means affect the ends; the end of wrong means is a big disappointment; happy results require right means.

A powerful position that is gained by trickery, deceit,

conniving, and backstabbing turns out to be a loss. Usually, when you step on somebody, it is a step back and you've had to look backward to do it. You've created a monster. Then you begin to feel that somebody might do the same to you. The *Ancient Mariner* of Coleridge's poem parallels this feeling.

> Like one that on a lonesome road
> Doth walk in fear and dread,
> And having once turned round, walks on,
> And turns no more his head;
> Because he knows a frightful fiend
> Doth close behind him tread.

Discoverers have right means at their disposal. They search for them, find them, deploy them, and exult as they do. Ultimately, if not sooner, they are exalted by them.

Get a Wastebasket

"This is my prayer, that your love may grow ever richer and richer in knowledge and insight of every kind, and may thus bring you the gift of true discrimination" [or may teach you what things are most worthwhile] (Philippians 1:9, NEB).

Get a big wastebasket—a mental wastebasket—and keep it close at hand, for the many times you will face decisions on what to pursue; what to take; what to eliminate.

One of the gripping events in A. J. Cronin's *The Citadel* illustrates this point. A young doctor, whose health proposals were defeated, became dejected and, in despair, sold his instruments and wasted the rest of his life as an alcoholic.

After his wife died, the doctor went through her things and found mementoes of earlier years. He found pictures of himself as a doctor; pictures of and letters from poor miners expressing their love for his tireless efforts on their behalf; pictures of young couples with infants cuddled in their arms—babies he had brought into this world. His wife had saved all of these—and more—to keep alive in her heart what he had once been and what he might have been.

Sensing that he had failed to use a mental wastebasket to eliminate the negative forces that plundered his life, the doctor realized that he had been fooling himself. In disgust he cried at himself, "You thought you were getting away with it, but you weren't!"

God has given you the faculty of decision; He offers you guidance for adequate choices each day and in every area of life He opens to you. This decision requires serious faith, diligent desire, confident humility, and steady action.

Usually, the process of addition constitutes, at the same time, some elimination. Use your mental waste-basket! Make good use of it! Wad up the trifles, which have your life bound in failure and frustration, and toss them into the wastebasket.

To a sprinter, one-hundredth of a second can make the difference between first and last place.

A single point can spell the difference between a game won or lost.

Little things cluttering your life can make the difference between sailing and sinking. In life, you may be like a sailboat or a steamboat—you can drift or take action.

Discoverers become steamboaters because they have the spirit of success. Someone said that the basic difference between failure and success is mental attitude. The honest Discoverer trusts in the Lord; has peace in his heart and mind; is poised in his thinking; is positive in his action.

God keeps you in complete *peace* when your mind is full of Him because you *trust* in *Him* (Isaiah 26:3).

Success today! Success always! Success in everything is *reality for Discoverers!*

LIFE-LIFTER

Discoverers are real people who succeed at living when they go through the night. They are becomers. Night experiences nudge them forward.

There's enough to meet every need!

When I was a boy, we played scrub. Do you know what scrub is and why it was played? Although scrub is very similar to softball — we used a ball, bats and gloves, and the positions are the same as in softball — it doesn't require a full team of nine players. With four boys — one to pitch, one to play infield, and two to bat — we were ready for a rip-roaring game of scrub.

MANY PEOPLE ARE LIVING SCRUB!

Unfulfilled lives dish out weak ideas, weak projects, weak attempts, and result in weak achievements. The reason is very clear; in one manner or another such persons are inculcated with a have-not psychology. They have a poor man's spirit and, consequently, they have not. They think little, act little, give little. Are you one of these persons?

During a conversation with my friend, Dr. Norman

Vincent Peale, he recounted the time his literature ministry was on the rocks. Dr. Peale is the sort of man who wants to use every method he can to spread the news of abundant living through our Lord Jesus Christ. In the late 1930s, he realized that the printed page can make a powerful impact, so he began to distribute Christian literature.

Although it is the Lord's work, it still requires money — sometimes large sums. Not yet off the ground, Dr. Peale found his new outreach ministry with a $100,000 deficit, and not one dime left!

It looked like the end. Everything was called to a standstill. Creditors were uneasy; the outlook was dark; hopes were down; spirits were dull.

Dr. Peale requested a few trusted friends to meet with him. The occasion was solemn and a funereal atmosphere prevailed. Gloom poured over the gathering like thick molasses, because everyone kept harping on the have-not line.

In addition to his friends, Dr. Peale had invited a lady who had given $2,000 to get the ministry started. He had high hopes that lightning would strike twice. It did, but not exactly as he had envisioned.

"Gentlemen," she began, when Dr. Peale asked if she had any suggestions, "I know why you have called me here. You want me to put up another sizable donation. Well, I have news for you . . . I'm not!"

Dr. Peale's face sank a foot. It was as if a ton of lead had been dropped on that assemblage.

"Because," she insisted, "you don't need my money as much as you need a spiritual transfusion." Then, as only a determined woman can, she lowered the boom. "You are thinking *lack,* and as long as you think that way, you'll lack."

She did something for them that day that raised not only the $2,000 that Dr. Peale had thought she might give, but tens of millions of dollars from hundreds of thousands of people over the next thirty years. She outlined how to think plenty, how to define the number of people they needed to become solvent and how to accomplish the ministry in coming years.

In that meeting, she prayed for spiritual surgery to be performed on those men, cutting away the have-not spirit; she prayed for a fresh implant of spiritual plenty.

"It changed my life," said Dr. Peale. It changed his ministry, underscored by the fact that it got them on their feet. And it has led them to a monthly ministry affecting almost 3 million families around the world.

When insufficient finances began to send cold doubts into me about the ministry, to which I definitely believe almighty God led me, a confidant said, "David, if you think poor, then uncertainties will frighten you, and you will find them all around you."

One of the most wonderful availabilities to you is the promise of plenty. The secret to having plenty is elementary yet revolutionary to daily life.

FOLLOW GOD'S PLAN FOR YOUR LIFE—DAY-BY-DAY—AND YOU'LL HAVE EVERYTHING YOU NEED!

Each of us has a choice: Living as a *king* or a *kink!* ". . . all who will take God's gift . . . are kings of life" (Romans 5:17, LB). You see, you may become a millionaire in living. You may become a Discoverer.

Have you ever had a kink in a chain or a line of string? A knot? When life is tied up in a knot, it is *kinky*. You are immobilized, at the very least, ineffectualized by it.

Hallmarks of kinky living are: problems defeat you; reality scares you; surprises sideline you; you depend on life-substitutes; you are half-hearted about life; life is more endurance than enjoyment.

But the *kingly* living of Discoverers results from following a higher life-plan each day. I have discovered *twelve advantages* to this kind of plentiful living.

WORRY IS TAKEN OUT OF NEEDS

Think of it — no more frantic, frenzied hurry that breaks down the body. No more ragged nerves from slaving to get enough; you will have enough at the time you need it. Getting ahead has a new meaning and produces a remarkable ease.

When a person has worry removed from needs:

He is filled with *living* energy. (He has energy for every requirement of life — I can do everything I am supposed to do through Christ who strengthens me.)

He is kept safe from defeat and disaster. (Each one is transformed into a stepping-stone and classroom.)

He is maintained in balance. (When he stumbles, he has what it takes to get up and go on.)

He sleeps without fear. (What rest and restoration!)

He is free from the *fear* of failure. (Although he is not free from failure.)

He is free from the *fear* of adversity and adversaries.

He is free from the *fear* of old age, retirement, loss of limb, senility, sickness, unemployment, unwantedness, and death.

He has fantastic *inner* power helping, pulling, pushing him.

YOU ARE RELEASED FROM KEEPING UP WITH THE JONESES

Somebody has said that everyone is born an original and dies a copy. Anyone who tries to keep up with the Joneses is copying.

Many of us are suffering from a loss of the *sense of self;* we have the "copy" disease. The individual is swallowed by the herd, and we move in a "herd-life."

Pushed by the crowd, some conform to conformity by keeping up with the Joneses—at least, they try frantically.

Others conform to nonconformity. At all costs, they keep away from keeping up with the Joneses. In the process, they create their own "Joneses" system.

In each case, it is living by a slave morality and mentality. It is underscored by dehumanization, often in the guise of finding oneself. In both instances, you lose your individuality—perhaps your personality. You feel you are insignificant and at the mercy of forces around you.

In this dreadful condition, you tend to become a performer rather than a person. You base self and dignity and success on acceptance more than worth. (What will *"they"* think?) As a result, you begin to act on random impulse.

What can you do? Become your own "Joneses." Otherwise, as Dr. M. E. Dodd explains, you are twisting a tune out of a hand organ when you could be playing a four-manual pipe organ. You are satisfied to play with mud pies when you could be making angel-food cakes. You are crawling when you could be running. You are sitting when you could be standing. You are building a shack when you could be building a palace.

You are in a shell. You need to break out and over-come this defeat! You need honest love in your heart — for yourself, too!

You may live with meaning! You may get a bang out of life, but you must become an original again — an honest-to-goodness individual. You must regather self.

NO MORE EMPTINESS

In *Man's Search for Himself,* Dr. Rollo May states that many of us do not know what we want and have no clear idea of how we feel. T. S. Eliot's "Hollow Men" describes modern America and multitudes of people throughout the world.

> We are the hollow men
> We are the stuffed men
> Leaning together
> Headpiece filled with straw. Alas!
> Shape without form, shade without colour,
> Paralysed force, gesture without motion. . . .
>
> T. S. ELIOT

But what is at the heart of this wrecking emptiness? I am convinced it stems from a loss of the *sense of the image of God* within.

We are made in His image. This is the consciousness which distinguishes men from monkeys. It is soul — a need for God, which is felt — and ability to respond.

Kafka, in *Metamorphosis,* depicts what happens spiritually to a person who doesn't sense and utilize the image of God. An empty young man lives an empty life as a salesman. He leaves his middle-class home every morning and returns every night; he eats the same roast beef every Sunday, while his father falls asleep at the table.

Life is boring and routine. His life is so empty that one morning the salesman wakes up and discovers that he is no longer a human being, he is a cockroach!

He has forfeited his image of God and become a cockroach—a leech living off crumbs left by others, with no distinctive self, no sense of God or need for God.

The image of God includes marvelous potentialities and possibilities. For example, some chimps have been sent into space, but chimps haven't sent men there—not a one! And rats have been used to verify the miracle drugs from the lab, but never has a rat made a single discovery.

The image needs to be activated; there is a loss of effect if you don't utilize it. What is its primary use? *To trust God with your life.*

When the spirit of plenty takes over, emptiness is banished! That nothingness feeling, which is completely unnecessary, fades away and is replaced by significance! You feel you are somebody and you have something big!

SHALLOWNESS IS ERASED

The roots go deep enough to get to the source and sustenance of every truly successful life.

Recently, a police officer phoned me after midnight and asked if I could come to the hospital emergency room to talk to a young man who had just attempted to take his life. When I got there, the doctor was sewing up the horrible slashes the man had inflicted. The physician assured me that it might be advantageous for both of us to work on the patient at the same time, so, as the doctor sewed up the outer wounds, I tried to get to the much deeper injuries in his heart.

"What does life mean to you?" I asked.

"Not much," he muttered. "I feel so shallow."

I have talked with many people who admit that they are only skimming the surface of life. They have come to the conclusion that there isn't much to life, because there isn't much to *their* lives.

The answer is enlightened discovery.

You will discover that your life is something to *ex*press, not *sup*press. Worthy of expression, you express *you* because *you* are filled and the *you* is wonderful! "They began to express themselves" (Acts 2:4, MOFFATT translation).

YOU OVERCOME SHABBINESS

You discover you always have enough regardless of how much *enough* is. Even more, you have the power to make it work.

As a Discoverer you

Accent what you have!
Adapt to what you have!
Use what you have!
Are grateful for what you have!

Amazingly, *this paves the way for more.* To the one who has, shall more be given.

YOU GET THE EDGE OVER
DISCOURAGEMENT

How often have you felt blue because of the have-nots? Debilitated spiritually, you assume a passive posture to circumstances—a give-in, give-up will and sometimes a me-too morality. Indefiniteness sets in, followed by confusion, lostness, wandering, polluted ambition, diluted values, anxiety, and lean goals—if any.

Several years ago, a man opened a little ten-stool cafe in Pasadena, California, and did surprisingly well. He expanded and opened another and then another. One proud day, he was able to send his only son to college. And, after the boy was graduated, the man took him in as a business partner.

"Dad," said the young man, "you know the country is undergoing a recession. Business is bad—really bad. Things are tough. We've got to cut back on advertising, reduce our inventory, and let some of our workers go. We must tighten our belts and pull in the reins."

Now, even though there was an economic slump, Dad had been doing better than ever. But his son was an educated man. He had taken courses in management and marketing, and he was the proud holder of a degree in Business Administration.

"You know," Dad thought, as he began to get discouraged, "Junior's got something. All this time, we've been in a slump and I didn't even know it!"

They began to cut back and cut down. Eventually, believe it or not, they closed up. Discouragement!

Discoverers have courage (at least, they get it), for their reliable source provides enough at every level, every day, for every occasion.

YOUR LIFE IS TURNED INTO A DONATION

You really have a lot to give — more than you may think! Bob McDonald is an example.

A 100-ton piece of delicate machinery needed to be relocated twenty-five feet away. The problem had everyone stumped, until Bob, a factory foreman, analyzed how it could be done.

Bob ordered a hundred pounds of bananas! "What's this?" his associates wondered. "Has he flipped?"

Bob had the machine tilted slightly, then he spread banana peels under it. Keeping the equipment intact, the men slid it easily to its new location.

As a Discoverer, you live on what you have rather than what you have not.

You give on what you have. Many give on what they have not, saying, "I don't have anymore to give. After all," they argue, "you can see what I have left when I've paid all the bills." But you have more to give than money. You have

ideas

faith

hope

love

energy

prayers

smiles

time

abilities

In addition, you will give on what you *will* have, since you are reinforced with a pledge of supply. The future doesn't baffle you. As a Discoverer you build on it!

LIFE-EMPHASIS IS PLACED ON
SIGNIFICANT VALUES

The spirit of plenty eliminates fuss about *things*. One may have possessions without plenty. One may have possessions *and* plenty. But, as a Discoverer, you move through every day anchored by hope and stabilized by a life-freeing presence of your God, whether you have much or little.

I never really knew my Grandmother Coffman, who passed away when I was a small boy. But I do remember Granny Ray. Her spritely, five-foot-two, 100-lb. frame was distinguished by a red complexion, auburn-red hair, and a capacity for life typical of the Lucas clan.

She was a farm woman from the rolling lands of Hill County, Texas. Although she was never known for extraordinary culinary ability, she did keep her family adequately fed. What sticks most in my mind about her are her values!

She had *persistence*. Granddad Jim Ray who made his way alone, from East Tennessee to Texas, as a thirteen-year-old boy, was a rugged, time-toughened, sometimes vociferous man. But more than once, her persistence wore him down and won him over—although the way over was occasionally marked with growling and scowling.

I remember also her *frugality and hard work*. Completely unpretentious, Granny knew how to get the last copper out of a penny. She had to—they didn't have much of this world's goods. Still, she shared willingly. More than once, she turned away from view and dipped her hand into a secret compartment for a well-creased twenty dollar bill to buy something for the grandkids. Her secret compartment was located somewhere inside the top of her cotton petticoat—her own safety deposit box—where she kept her milk and egg earnings, clamped by a big safety pin.

Often, as they sped down the narrow dusty road by our place on their way home from the traditional Saturday expedition to town, Granny would toss a sack of candy over the wire fence. Behind that fence, in a red rocking chair, sat a pudgy, freckled-face little grandson named David, who plotted the rendezvous carefully, in order to get a jump on two older brothers and a younger sister!

But, even more impressive was the *simple faith* that charted her life. I do not mean the faith of a simpleton, or, a moronic belief. I mean the kind of faith you and I need—a faith in Christ that is dynamic, life-changing, directing, renewing, reinforcing, and expanding: a faith that is free from complexities; a faith that is workable *now;* a faith that does something creative and thrilling about those problems you're up against. Some people have such a mechanized and complex faith it seems neither relevant nor practical. And their lives are snarled up.

Also, Granny had a *love for the Bible* that made the stories of Samuel, Saul, David, Gideon, and Samson come alive, when she told them to us, as we sat at her knee.

Her *prayers* were equally powerful — not sophisticated, just honest and weighty with meaning — as was her *church membership* and *faithful attendance*. Rain, shine, cold, or heat, Granny made her way four or five miles to the country church.

She was a Discoverer!

YOU HAVE A NEW VITALITY

Worry, the "Joneses" philosophy, hollowness, shabbiness, and discouragement make people sick — literally!

Experts claim that the day is rapidly approaching when two-thirds of all hospital beds in America will be filled by people with emotional problems.

In the last hundred years, the population of the United States increased over eight times; institutionalized mental patients have increased some 25,000 times!

We have greater knowledge about such matters now than we did a hundred years ago, and people are more prone to seek professional help now than a hundred years ago. The demands of life today are much greater than they were a hundred years ago. Still the statistics are staggering.

The spirit of plenty is the answer!

No respecter of age, generation, race, or class — it sweeps out such producers of illness. It has tremendous healing power!

KEEP LIFE EXCITING

Each day is a new beginning. It is actually possible for you to awake in the morning with a ringing affirmation: "Lord, it will be great to see how You meet my needs today." The question is no longer *if* they will be met — you have gone beyond that stage. It has become a matter of *how*, for you are assured of an answer adequate to the need.

There is an answer to *every* need! Thomas Edison had the right idea when he said that what man's mind can create, man's character can control.

MAKES YOU A WHOLE, REAL PERSON

You are a *human* being—with faults. Human beings make mistakes and have disappointments.

The spirit of plenty takes your humanity into account, then encourages a program of daily growth from which you can find a great deal of satisfaction.

The spirit of plenty helps you accept what you cannot change and to keep your head high. It helps you laugh at miscues to go on living.

The spirit of plenty doesn't expect you to be God, nor does it allow you to be an animal.

An actor once said, "Every man has to have a reason to get up in the morning." The spirit of plenty gives you the reason. Someone who enjoys sleeping late may mumble, "Yes, but man doesn't have to get up *early!*" Early or late, you have *reason*, and you feel it.

PROVIDES MOTIVATION

If you are sufficiently motivated, you can tackle whatever you face; live up to your potential; and develop your possibilities. When you are motivated, you may accomplish what you thought impossible.

Late one evening, a man took a shortcut through the cemetery and, accidentally, fell into a newly dug grave. He tried so hard to climb out that he exhausted himself completely and had to give up. Exasperated, he settled

down in a corner to wait for daylight. Just as he dozed
off, a teen-ager, hurrying home from his girl friend's
house, fell into the same grave.

Unaware of the man's presence, the young fellow tried
to get out. He grunted and groaned, giving it everything
he had. The predicament looked hopeless. Then the man
reached over and tapped the boy on the shoulder.
"Might as well give up, sonny," he said, "I couldn't get
out either." But the teen-ager did. He was motivated!

Motivation is a tremendous force. It is a deep longing
that transfers itself into drive. The drive, in turn, trans-
lates itself into action. Then the course motivation
follows is: *desire . . . drive . . . deed.* What does this
mean?

One who says he wants to become a Christian and
doesn't, isn't sufficiently motivated. The young person
who claims he wants peace in his heart and doesn't
have it, isn't motivated enough. The senior citizen who
says he is tired of boredom and dull days, and still
tolerates them, isn't motivated enough.

The businessman who claims he wants to get ahead on
honest-to-goodness principles and continues in his old
ways is not motivated enough. The troubled couple who
boast they want their marriage to work, yet it doesn't, is
not motivated sufficiently. You may be thinking, "There's
more to life than what I'm experiencing." You are right.
There is. And if you aren't moving out to the fuller,
happier life, you're bogged down with insufficient motivation. Anybody who wants to join the church and
doesn't, isn't motivated enough. The person who feels
he wants the wonderful blessings tithing opens to him,
and still isn't tithing, is not yet motivated significantly.

Life moves on motivation. Positive action *always*

results from deep desire plus drive. When there is a fervent burning in your spirit — "a fire" as it was described by one man — something is going to happen. ". . . What things soever ye desire when ye pray, believe . . ." (Mark 11:24, KJV).

A very bright and prosperous man shared his experience with me. When he finally realized that money and a going business aren't all there is to life, he began to attend church regularly. What he heard touched him — "got home," he said.

"I assured myself that what I needed was membership. I came to a membership meeting, heard everything you said, and I agreed. On a Sunday, I stood in front of this sanctuary cross and professed faith. But I suppose it was more talk than fact, on my part."

(Church membership without a vital and active faith will leave a person stalled.)

"Then I began to listen deep in my heart," he continued.

"What happened then?" I asked him.

"Well, I started getting motivated in a new way. It seemed to me that Jesus Christ was to live in my life seven days each week rather than one." The more he heard and read, the more he wanted to have his week filled with Christ. "When I thought I couldn't stand the urge any longer, I asked God to get deep in my heart and have His way. 'God,' I prayed, 'I give You my life,' and God took it." Now, that man is really growing and glowing as a Christian, and the church means more than ever to him.

Desire plus drive equals deed. When there is enough desire, drive will find a way. As Dick Hillis put it, we only truly believe that which activates us.

You may be wondering how to get motivated enough. Fear isn't big enough to really do it; neither is punishment. *Need* is a good motivator; so is *opportunity;* and a *worthy objective* helps.

Remember the Greatest Motivator ever known is Jesus Christ.

LIFE-LIFTER

Your need is an opportunity. There is a source of supply equal to the need — ALWAYS!

I can win over worry— in this life

Robert Lee Frost, the American poet, claimed that man is a funny thing. When he hasn't got anything else on earth to worry about, he goes off and gets married. I know a desperate mother of eight who insists that is when a person's worries really begin. After the surprising arrival of number eight, someone asked what she wants her next one to be, and she replied, "A grandchild!"

The truth is, we live in a worried world.

People are worrying about

the church,

the environment,

the Establishment,

the family,

the government,

nations,

people,

philosophies,

the "power structure,"

the status quo,

themselves,

vanishing values,

and youth.

If you are overreacting, you can sympathize with British philosopher Bertrand Russell who commented on the painful thing of these times: "Those who feel certainty are stupid, and those with any imagination and understanding are filled with doubt and indecision."

You are worried. It will be good for you to face worry forthrightly, for what it really is — *a stream of fear in your mind.* It may be a thin trickle slipping through or a wide, unrestricted flood on a rampage.

But for what purpose? If you will test previous worries intelligently and spiritually, you will arrive at the same conclusion that I have — most of them never happen. One man stated, "Don't tell me that worry doesn't do any good. I know better. The things I worry about don't happen."

Discoverers win over worry, because they develop a peaceful mental attitude which breaks the will of worry at its base. Then, the advice from the Bible, "Don't worry about anything . . ." (Philippians 4:6, LB) is livable.

GET TO WORK

A man said he doesn't have anything to worry about. "My wife takes care of the money, and my mother-in-law tends to my business. All I have to do is work." It is a fact that honest work decreases worry. As the work meter goes up, the worry meter goes down.

According to Robert Frost, the reason that worry kills more people than work is that more people worry than work.

Too many people have too much time to worry because they spend too little time actually working — on and off the job!

A labor consultant advised one company that their employees were rabid clock watchers. At five o'clock, there was an hysterical flight from work.

Why? Possibly because people do not understand the creative contribution work may be to life. Work is a productive and rewarding use of time, and *time is a commodity entrusted to you.* It is of immense value, consequently the Bible reminds you often to make the most of it.

Discoverers are motivated to work. (This desire is backed up by energy.) They have work made available to them, for the Discoverer will find an opening. He never gives up in his search. One turndown stimulates him to try again. Tempted to feel "what's the use?" he draws on resources far superior to discouragement. The peace which is growing in his heart keeps him going until he discovers his place.

Like Paul, he believes he has a work to do — each one does — you, too! "God has given each of us the ability to do certain things well . . ." (Romans 12:6, LB). And he finds it and does it, diligently.

To me it is clear: *You are a human being, not a mattress.* Work activity is a donation to your well-being! Worklessness is a drain on it!

KEEP WORK AT WORK!

Dr. Herbert Herschner, a physician and friend, once told me, "Occasionally you may take your work home with you and get by with it. But when you take your worries home with you from work, you will never get by with it!"

The Discoverer's peace, giving you an adequate use of those seconds, minutes, and hours, enables you to work on your work, whether at home or at the job. Work — not worry! And it balances the time so that you will not overdo. Even more significant, the Discoverer's peace will keep worry out of work at home or on the job. *Peace keeps worry out of YOU — wherever you are!*

PARTICIPATE IN LIFE

Worry jams life processes; it takes a person out of living. If worry persists, you will feel like Abraham Lincoln who, in the darkest hours of the Civil War, was quoted as saying, "If there's a worse place than hell, I am in it."

WORRY WILL TAKE THE LIFE OUT OF LIVING OR LIVING WILL TAKE THE WORRY OUT OF LIFE!

It buries your participation in life prematurely.

I have an acquaintance who is thirty-eight years of age and, for the last ten years, he has lived through a thousand deaths — all imaginary. Although he has not suffered a heart attack, much of the time he thinks he's going to have one at any moment. His life sphere is very small indeed.

"I can't do this. . . . I can't do that. . . . I can't; my condition, you know."

At best, he runs on one-fourth steam. And he may bring on an attack!

Dr. John Haldane, the English scientist, observed that he has never met a healthy person who worried very much about his health.

That isn't hard to figure out. Worries break one's health.

The famous American surgeon, Dr. Charles Mayo (founder of the clinic in Minnesota), spoke from personal experience when he said that worry affects the circulation—the heart, the glands, the whole nervous system. He added, "I have known many who died from worry."

Chaplain Peter Marshall shocked that dignified gathering of United States Senators when he prayed that we be saved from the sin of worrying, lest stomach ulcers be the badge of our faith.

Dr. Rollo May, the prominent psychoanalyst, insisted that worry is our modern form of the great white plague —the greatest destroyer of human health and well-being.

Worry disfigures your appearance. Many people eat themselves fat over anxiety. I was told of a man who went from 185 pounds to 475 pounds from worrying. He stopped worrying and he's on the way back to 185— presently, he is an impressive 265! Disraeli said that worry steals the bloom from the cheek and lightness from the pulse. It turns the hair gray.

But *peace flings open the doors to life, by closing the doors on worry.* Discoverers have a zing about life and a zip for life. With sleeves rolled up, they wade into life, giving it what they've got, and, believe me, they've got something!

Have you ever studied the origin of the word "worry"? It comes from an old Anglo-Saxon term meaning "to choke," and that it does! *It freezes the mind, hardens your emotional arteries, and cuts off your spiritual circulation.*

Soon, *things* begin to worry you.

A man who lost his job when the company went into an austerity program lost everything he had mortgaged, which, in the tradition of modern America, was everything he had. That put him in a position where *things* no longer worried him. "I am so poor," he said, "that I really cannot afford to let anything worry me." At last, he made things adapt to *him* rather than adapt his life to things.

GET TOUGH MENTALLY

You must have a peaceful mental outlook to face realities at times. It is grit-stuff, which successful living requires.

"I found out I had to be tough mentally," a man remarked, "when I was out for a job." There were two possibilities; he felt a strong urge to pursue one of them. Prayer played a big part in it. But he found out that MT (mental toughness) was necessary.

"I couldn't get any further than the receptionist," he said, "until I practiced MT." Persistence paid off—and persistence is a display of MT. From the outset, God had given him a marvelous sense of peace. Regardless of the outcome, he knew he would be a winner.

"I'm not surprised at what is happening here," said a new family, in reference to our church's dynamic and far-reaching ministries. Our church in San Dimas has MT; therefore, it doesn't let ups and downs rough it up. Every church needs MT! So does every minister! With

MT, God will perform amazing feats through both!

You're a human being. And, as a human being, you are a *mistake-maker*. Everyone of us is. If you were perfect, people couldn't stand you! You couldn't stand yourself! And you couldn't stand God, because no longer would you feel a need for Him.

Since you are a mistake-maker, you will worry yourself to death unless you become a *mistake-breaker*. Discoverer's peace, with the MT it produces, transforms mistake-makers into mistake-breakers. Then, Discoverers aren't buried in a tomb of error; they blossom in a triumph of ecstasy from their errors.

RELEASE A RESILIENT SPIRIT IN YOUR LIFE

Unbendable people are breakable people. Living often calls for bounce-back — one of the victories one may gain through a setback.

A man in my area faced the biggest crisis of his life. His high aims and great ideals looked as though they were crashing in on him. Projects seemed dashed; hopes doomed.

A co-worker, who was fully aware of the situation, said, "I don't understand him. His world is falling apart, yet *he* isn't. He's not even perturbed, actually. Maybe," insisted this fellow worker, "he doesn't fully realize what's happening."

"How's that?" I asked.

"He told me that if these doors close, there are others somewhere else and we'll find them."

The man relating this incident could hardly believe his ears. "He claims that God has a place for these dreams. It's a case of finding it."

That's the Discoverer's spirit — undefeating, undefeatable, unrelenting, and unsinkable! Great people have possessed it down through the years; Paul had it in his heart.

Remember how he wanted to take the Christian gospel to Bithynia? How much he wanted to go into that nerve center of the ancient world? He tried, but the door was closed.

Instead of crying about it, he led his party courageously into other opportunities, which opened to them. Thank God! Because of that, western civilization has been influenced by the message of faith, hope, and love.

If one of life's doors closes, there's a better one somewhere.

When a door is shut, it is, in itself, a guide post to something better.

Not every door is the door for *you*.

Most doors in life need nudging.

The right door will open to you.

Pray; believe; push; pray; believe.

A resilient spirit is necessary to experience this wholeness of life. Worry causes cold rigidity. Are you to be a rubber stamp — always bending, scraping, bowing? No! Definitely not!

How may you know when to bend?

Ask God what He wants in the matter you face.

Consider the alternatives. When General Dayan, head of Israel's Air Force in the "Six Day War of 1967," was asked what secondary plan of attack they had if their primary attack failed, he replied that they had none, the first one had to work. Sometime you may be locked in a life or death struggle, and your one and only strategy *must* work. Usually, however, you have alternatives. What are they? You must evaluate them and be conclusive.

Principles, morality, and ethics require firmness and determination. No resilience must be, or needs to be, tolerated there.

PUT PROBLEMS IN POSITIVE FOCUS

When you feel powerless before the onrush of problems, you get worrisome. One outstanding doctor related that worry is the feeling of being caught and overwhelmed. Instead of becoming sharper, our perceptions become blurred and vague.

Worry magnifies minuses and minimizes majors. It empties the day of its strength, and disqualifies you from meeting your problems dynamically. Worry pushes out the plus within, and pushes in the problems from without.

Years ago, Paul worried, too. "I don't understand myself at all, for I really want to do what is right, but I can't. . . . I know perfectly well that what I am doing is wrong. . . . But I can't help myself. . . . No matter which way I turn I can't make myself do right. I want to but I can't" (Romans 7:15, 16, 17, 18, LB).

You must set those problems in their place. Even though they may not shake the world, they have something to do with shaping *your* world!

I am fortunate to have a number of wonderful friends in Florida. One day I received a letter from two of them — Mr. and Mrs. Pete Wecker, an elderly couple in St. Petersburg — who told me the circumstances of their first meeting at a senior citizen's program at the church. Still capable of a great amount of love, they were attracted to each other, and Pete invited her out to dinner and a movie. During the show, he bent over to look for something on the floor.

She whispered, "What have you lost?"

"A caramel," he answered.

She began to wonder about the ability of her new flame to make a sensible judgment!

"Why go to all this trouble for a caramel?" she asked.

"Because my teeth are in it."

In a way, the problem shaped *his* world. She didn't let it get the best of her. She married him anyway. That's keeping it in positive focus!

Peace really does work in this regard. It is clearly outlined in the Bible.

> . . . we can have real peace with Him [God] because of what Jesus Christ our Lord has done for us (Romans 5:1, LB).
>
> We can rejoice, too, when we run into problems and trials for we know that they are good for us—they help us learn to be patient (v. 3).
>
> And patience develops strength of character in us and helps us trust God each time until finally our hope and faith are strong and steady" (v. 4).

PUT SLEEP IN YOUR NIGHT

Tossing and turning, the night is drained of its creative, restorative process. Sleep is a cure for waking troubles, as Cervantes points out, but worry keeps the troubles fermenting. Charged up, the mind becomes a fitful storm.

> It is not the work, but the worry
> That drives all sleep away,
> As we toss and turn and wonder
> About the cares of the day.

Do we think of the hand's hard labor
Or the steps of the tired feet?
Ah, no! But we plan and wonder
How to make both ends meet.
— ANONYMOUS

Discoverers have the assurance that God truly cares for them; therefore, they place their cares of life on Him.

At the end of the day, they may confidently affirm: "O Christ, my life is in Your big hands. So is _____, _____, _____, _____, and every care I have. If you want me to be taken to Your home this night, I shall never awake to another dawn here. If You still have something wonderful for me to do in this life, I shall welcome the dawn with enthusiasm. Whichever and whatever, You are my Guide and Friend. I commit my body and mind to the sleep You have promised me. Goodnight, God."

Nicky Cruz is one of the most remarkable converts from an unbelievable life of terror to beauty and love that I have ever met. Art Linkletter says that faith and God's power literally deprived crime of a key leader. Nicky shared his story on one of our inspirational telecasts.

As a boy, Nicky's mother told him that the devil had picked him for a hellish life. Born in Puerto Rico, he was only thirteen years of age when he was banished from his home and made his way to New York City. He soon came to the conclusion that the ghetto was a jungle and, if he wanted to survive, he must live by the laws of that jungle.

Soon, Nicky became a notorious gang member, and he introduced some new laws to the jungle. Vicious and mean, he gained a reputation for his fierce fighting. "Nicky baby doesn't lose," he said.

Then he became head of the Mau Mau's — the toughest gang in the jungle.

"I'm really ashamed to talk about it," Nicky said, as he reminisced. Stabbing, brutal beatings, dope, rape, fear, and intimidation — this was his life.

"I had no future. I lived only for the day. I didn't look to live past twenty anyhow," he claimed.

But one day, the tough-shelled young man was assured by a tough-minded preacher, "Nicky, Jesus loves you."

"I spit on him, said I could kill him, and told him to go to _____."

"Nicky," guaranteed the preacher, "Jesus loves you. You can cut me up in a thousand pieces. Still, Jesus loves you."

This talk got to the gang leader. Inside, he knew his life was a bitter hypocrisy. Besides, someone had looked him in the eye — him, the ferocious, embattled, "devil-stricken" Nicky Cruz — and dauntlessly claimed that Jesus loved him.

"Nobody ever loved me before."

The upshot of it was the conversion of Nicky to Jesus Christ.

"I dropped to my knees and asked this Jesus to take over my messed-up life and to forgive me."

He was reborn!

"Oh," he glowed, as he tried to convey his feelings to me and to millions of viewers, "it happened here — here!" He motioned to his heart.

"Such joy! I had never been happy! Never in my life! Always misery! But then I was happy!

"And love. For the first time in my whole life, I felt love. And peace — what an ease. No more fighting in my heart. For the first time in years, I went to bed without fear of somebody shooting me through the window, or crashing in and stabbing me to death, or beating me to death.

"Nicky wasn't the same guy.

"Nicky was a new man from that day.

"I closed my eyes that night and said, 'God, thank You.'

"Goodnight, Jesus.

"And I slept like a baby!"

RENEW GENUINE APPRECIATION FOR YOURSELF

Centuries ago, Pascal felt that the reason many people of his day went wild over diversions was that the *diversions enabled people to avoid thoughts about themselves*.

Diversions make a person lose the deeper concept of himself—who he is (a creation of almighty God), what he is (a human being), where he is (in a real world), what he may become (possibilities unlimited through Jesus Christ), and where he is going—an appreciation for himself.

We may learn a lesson from the seven-year-old, second-grader in Tennessee who wrote an essay entitled, "My face":

"My face has two brown eyes. It has a nose and two cheeks. And two ears and a mouth. I like my face. I'm glad that my face is just like it is. It is not bad, it is not good, but just right."

That is the way my Uncle Mark thought of himself. His nose made Jimmy Durante's look like a molehill up against a mountain, but he insisted appreciatively, "It's mine. All mine."

This appreciation is positive humility!

In *Man's Search for Himself,* Dr. Rollo May reaffirms that conceit is the opposite of self-appreciation; rather, self-inflation is usually the sign of emptiness and self-doubt. Such false pride is one of the most common covers for worry.

Sören Kierkegaard dealt with it when he wrote: "If anyone, therefore, will not learn from Christianity to love *himself* in the right way, then neither can he love his neighbor. To love one's self in the right way and to love one's neighbor are absolutely analogous concepts, and are at bottom one and the same. Hence the law is: 'You shall love yourself as you love your neighbor when you love him as yourself.'"

> . . . be a new and different person with a fresh newness in all you do and think. . . . be honest in your estimate of yourselves, measuring your value by how much faith God has given you (Romans 12:2-3, LB).

Peace reinforces and practicalizes a divinely-initiated, Jesus-extending, life-effecting and electrifying, soul-deep appreciation for yourself. Gratefully, you may make the Discoverer's Pledge:

> God gave me, me.
>
> I am something big to God.
>
> I have something from God to do with my life today.
>
> I am forever.
>
> Therefore, I cannot afford second-class living.

REGAIN YOUR SELFHOOD

I heard a speaker state that the present typical American character is *outer-directed*. He seeks not so much to be outstanding as to *fit in*. He lives as though he is directed by a radar set clipped to his heart, which is constantly dictating to him what other people expect of him. He is like the man who never knew who he really was.

He has lost his selfhood — *his awareness as a unique person, his special touch as an individual.*

In an attempt to break out of his fit-in life, a local bus driver in a large city put his passengers out and turned from the route he traveled day after day. He headed south — bus plus driver — and ended up in Texas, 2,000 miles from home, where he spent a few days rollicking and relaxing.

But the transit officials filed charges against him, and officers arrested the bus driver and took him back home. When he arrived, several thousand people greeted him with a rousing ticker-tape welcome. They acknowledged that however ill-conceived and ill-fated his outbreak might have been, it was a search for selfhood.

Discoverer's peace, in a sensible manner, restores selfhood. "Don't copy the fashions and customs of this world . . ." (Romans 12:2, LB). Your direction comes from God, then you set behavior patterns and customs!

STEP IN THE SPIRIT OF JESUS CHRIST

Do not worry about *anything.* Pray about *everything.* (Sentence prayers are effective wherever you are.) Speak to God about what you need. Share — He's listening. And give God thanks for the answers — before they are received, while they are being received, and after they have been received.

Jesus did all of these things. You're in His Spirit by doing them.

Then you will *experience* further the *peace of God*—indescribable, it is so tremendous! He will keep your thinking in peace; your heart in peace; your life in peace, for you are *trusting* in Him and *God* is *fail-free!* This is His Spirit in you!

I assure you of this peace beginning *today—now!* You need not wait for a better time. *Now is the better time!*

10 COMMANDMENTS FOR WORRIERS

1) I will remember that worry is *unnatural* for me—a child of God. (It is natural for everyone who lives apart from faith and the power of Christ!)
2) I will be free from worry—it's up to *me!*
3) I will live this day. (It is the only day I have—at the moment!)
4) I will attend to troublesome developments as they arise. (Never harbor a grudge!)
5) I will not take worries to bed with me. (If I have any lingering at bedtime, I will commit them to their grave!)
6) I will pray for those who, knowingly or unknowingly, do me harm. (I will immediately become better; they may have a turnabout!)
7) I will let others help me. (Make sure it is help and not rule!)
8) I will do the best I know to do.
9) I will depend on the Lord for relief.
10) I will thank You, God.

LIFE-LIFTER

Worry whittles away at living and adds to your problem. Discoverers realize that life is rough at times; but when the way gets rugged, the rugged find a way.

FOURTH DISCOVERY

Tranquility without tranquilizers and tantrums

If you had one wish, what would it be?

Suppose it was for anything you want. Stretch your imagination, now. A million dollars? A palatial summer home? A prestigious job? I venture to guess that it may be for tranquility, for I have yet to hear a person say he doesn't want tranquility.

Although the heart and mind, even life as a whole, appeal for tranquility, many people are without it, or they have honest tranquility only by the spoonful. Where are they seeking it?

TRANQUILIZERS

Tranquilizers can be dangerous. An Indiana dog-catcher learned this fact firsthand, when he tried to capture a big German shepherd. As you know, tranquilizers are sometimes used to subdue animals, and, in his frantic efforts to get the dog, the dogcatcher dropped his tranquilizer gun and it discharged. Where do you suppose the dart hit? The neck of the dogcatcher! Observers say he felt simply heavenly for hours; his wife says he was never easier to get along with!

A senior citizen confided to me, "In the last year, I haven't talked to a person over fifty-five years of age who doesn't take tranquilizers or dope of some kind. That includes me," he confessed. "We carry them in our pockets for quick availability. Women carry them in their purses. They take the stuff with them everywhere they go."

"Why?" I asked. "Why do they feel a need for them?"

"Oh, boredom, I guess. Sitting around this house all day is misery."

Do something worthwhile! Don't waste your life lounging around the house all day. There's more to living than that! *If you will invest your time as God wants you to do, you're alive as long as you're breathing!* If you don't, you're a breathing mummy!

"And uselessness," the old man added. "We don't feel we're doing any good to anybody. Weakness must have something to do with it. We let ourselves slump to a point where we either refuse to face life or we're too anemic mentally and morally to stand up to it."

We have an epidemic! In a futile search for tranquility, young people are also looking to pills.

At a White House gathering, John Ingersoll, who, as Director of the Bureau of Narcotics & Dangerous Drugs, is in charge of 1,000 agents, said, "At most, we have 10 years to prevent a social catastrophe, if it is not too late already." Another leader spoke of drugs as a "cancer in our society" and that the spread of it is with lightning speed and intensity "among the young, in colleges, in businesses, and the military." "We have an epidemic on our hands," said Dr. Ambrose, "that can produce an American disaster." President Nixon told the conclave that the heart of the problem is in the human spirit and motivation. He assured them that if there is an answer, religion has it. Dr. Bertram Brown, Director of the National Institute of Mental Health, agrees that the answer is for people to turn on to life meaningfully rather than with a chemically induced haze.

I heard a teen-ager say that he needs pills to bring his mind together. "They give me personality." But where are the youth being influenced to experiment with pills? Often in Mother's and Dad's medicine cabinet, or bar, or pack. Do not discount the power of environment.

Oscar Ameringer, M.D. said, "Except that I inherited certain characteristics from an unknown number of unknown ancestors, I was deeply influenced by persons most of whom were dead before I was born, and shaped by circumstances over which I had no control, I am a self-made man."

Of course, there is more to it than Dr. Ameringer's explanation. Adults need not direct a hotline of condemnation at "this misguided generation," when the source may be behind their own noses. The world has plenty of old-time Davids who attempt to fix responsibility outside themselves.

A fifth-grade youngster at our school was taken to the principal's office because he walked into class stoned on pills. Immediately, we began to think a pusher was working this elementary school. "Horrible," some said indignantly. "What sort of a human being would sell or give stuff to kids?" When we got to the source of supply, what do you suppose it was? Dad's pills from Dad's bathroom!

You have two legs to stand on! And, boys and girls, young men and young women, on them you must stand! You are a person for yourself — an individual. There is also a big, big God who will help you stand strong, and tall, and straight — even if the example set before you is puny.

One of the brightest businessmen in Los Angeles, and a very dedicated Christian man, had a shiftless, lazy drifter for a father, and his mother was a hopeless alcoholic. But, as a young man, he stepped ahead of his surroundings and, by faith, he amazed those who knew about his background.

When you put your hand in the hands of Christ, it's up and away for you, if you want it to be! Your possibilities are fantastic and they can explode in richness, depth and purpose when they are detonated by the spirit of Christ in your heart and mind.

"I'm kicking pills . . . now!" says Johnny Cash in an article from *Guideposts* magazine, "I'm a free man now." The popular entertainment personality shares how pills led him to the left edge of life. After spending more time staring at the ceiling and fighting off sickness than he cares to mention, he got his fill of it. "I took pep pills to turn me on enough to do a show. Then I took depressants to calm down enough to get some sleep." Friends explained that Johnny was working too hard, traveling too much, and trying to jam too much into one day.

"I knew better

"The high they gave me was beautiful. I felt I owned the world," he said. "I stayed on pills because they made me feel great."

But then the truth began to break through. The highs weren't high enough anymore. Even though he increased the dosage from a few to several, and from several to dozens, Johnny was still moody, tense, nervous, and edgy. "That old feeling wasn't there. I didn't want to eat. I couldn't sleep. I started losing weight. So I went on depressants . . . looking for peace." What little he found he couldn't enjoy because he knew it was pill-controlled, therefore, illusory and momentary.

You tell me that's an answer to life's questions and needs? That's agony! Dr. William C. Dement of Stanford University claims that these pills bring on a tolerance that requires more pills. They interfere with normal sleep. Also they cause nightmares, anxiety, and even convulsions.

Not every pill-taker is in as serious a predicament as Johnny Cash was. I am sure, however, that there are some surprises in the executive pill closets of America. It might be embarrassing for someone else to open those doors and look in!

Pills to pull you up! Pills to pull you down! Pills to pull you in! Pills to pull you out! Pills to pull you through! Pills to pull you over! Pills to pull you under! Pills to improve your appearance! Pills to make you compatible! Pills to face life! Pills to forget life! Pills to dull your feeling! Pills to give you feeling! Pills to help you accept the cost of your pills without coming unraveled! (A senior-citizen friend pointed to the bill for a supply of pills — $134.00!) And the super-duper pill, the pill of all pills, the "Pill's Pill": the pill to erase the nausea of all other pills and get you back to where you started — reality!

"I'm kicking pills, as of now," Cash told his wife and

some friends. He decided to "give God's temple [body, mind, and spirit] back to Him." Thank God! Prayer pushed him through. Hypnotic suggestion, Freudian analysis, warm baths, massages, diets, exercise, and diversions often help, but the Power Center for tranquility is *God!*

TANTRUMS

In a search for tranquility, some people try tantrums reasoning, "I have to have an outlet, a release; otherwise I fly apart within." This reasoning is based on the philosophy that a person needs to blow his lid once in a while to ease the pressure. "After all" you think, "the tantrum is over in a minute." A shotgun blast is, too, but it blows everything to pieces. Things happen that tempt us to throw a tantrum. A woman said it was her husband coming in late at night. She found a way to get him home earlier and save a scene. One night, when Frank tiptoed cautiously in, she called in a loud whisper, "Harry, oh, Harry, is that you?"

But, at times, the pressure mounts like April 15th, and the tax deadline. There's a feeling-quake. Rumblings of a mental volcano — eruption imminent! Then we bawl and squall, figuratively speaking. A marriage counselor I know encourages people to let it blow. In fact, he advises couples to fight creatively. But I am positive there is a better way. Why am I sure? God!

Why waste energy on blowups? He did not give you life to waste energy on blowups! Suppose for a moment that there is, actually, some therapeutic value to a tantrum — that tension, pressure, frustration, torpedoed dreams, and the like, find a creative outlet through a fit.

The tantrum is OK, but still it is less than best. Even if some good were to come out of it, the rage leaves a person short of the satisfaction his spirit craves. The heart wants harmony. A blowup causes a blowout—disharmony! *Whatever good the tantrum might do, God can do better.* The happiness and composition the Almighty brings into a believing life far outweighs the best the tantrum can give.

God-Power produces balance! It doesn't leave you limp, sorry, ashamed, disgusted with yourself, and blue. With your head high, your spirit vital, your face beaming, your heart confident, and a proud feeling tingling every nerve of your makeup, you claim humbly, "God and I did it. No outburst—rather an uplift! No crash—instead a consummation! No fury—rather a fullness! No sorrow—instead a sweetness! No curse—rather a cure!"

"God and I did it!"

What causes a gap in tranquility?

THE CONSCIOUS AND THE SUBCONSCIOUS

Experts tell us that one-tenth of your mind is conscious and nine-tenths is subconscious. Like an iceberg, much of what makes up the mind is below the surface. Noted Doctor David Abrahamsen says there is a conflict between the conscious and subconscious (or unconscious) mind, and the tension there must be reduced. Unless there is peace between them (at least enough peace), a human being experiences little tranquility. Unresolved hate, fear, revenge, and similar emotions drop into the subconscious; then they pop up in thoughts and actions. They may burst into violent dreams or nightmares when you sleep. Without an answer, problems slip into the subconscious; then they may show themselves through nervousness and tension.

There is power in your subconscious. The subconscious affects your life in proportion to its size. If nine-tenths of our mind is subconscious, amazing power is represented there—for good or bad. For example, the chances are that the man you chose for a husband or the woman you selected as a wife has something that attracted you from your subconscious level—a characteristic: looks; voice; hairstyling; a personality like a favorite aunt, or mother, or father. Possibly you look at your partner now, wondering what made you do it. Your sentiments may be expressed adequately by the sign at a church rummage sale which read: "Your chance to rid your house of everything not worth keeping, but too valuable to throw away. Bring your husband." If so, mark it to your subconscious.

It may be controlled! But do not make the error of taking the fatalistic view of the subconscious as some psychiatrists and psychologists have, claiming that everything one thinks, says, and does is determined by something over which one has no control. The subconscious directs, yes; but, in turn, it may be directed. It controls, but it may be controlled.

The subconscious can be, and needs to be, converted, too!

1) Consciously, put it in the Lord's hands. (Although you are in an area—the subconscious—that may be a mystery to you, the light of Christ will increasingly bring it to positive ends. He fully knows the way through it.)
2) Face problems when they come up. (Don't hide them, thus forcing them into the subconscious.)

3) Deal with ill feelings at their outset. (This will keep them from festering and filtering into the subconscious.)

4) Dispose of negative emotions like fear, hate, and revenge at once. (Get them off your chest then! It isn't a wish-out, but a wash-out that will get them off your back.)

Remember that Jesus said that a house ". . . divided against itself cannot stand" (Matthew 12:25, LB).

CONSIDER THE NEGATIVE CONCEPT OF COMPETITION

Another force leading to disruption is a negative concept of competition. I believe in rivalry that challenges the highest and best in men — but always in the spirit of goodwill. When jealousy, resentment and bitterness creep into competition, negative forces plant their feet in the heart and sow seeds of defeat.

As I write this book, I am also minister of a six-year-old, walk-in, drive-in congregation. It isn't the only one of its kind, nor is it the largest parish of the walk-in, drive-in churches. If I know my heart, there is no jealousy toward my colleagues at other churches, just a God-bless-them feeling and a determination to become the brightest light I can, where I am.

Other ministers have written books that have sold millions of copies. Mine haven't! But I am grateful for the help my writings have been to people; and I shall keep on writing as long as I believe God is guiding me. At the same time, I am very thankful that the books written by other ministers have given hope and courage to people.

I am involved in a TV ministry. Other religious telecasts are on many more stations, and get much more mail, and have a much larger income than ours, at this time. Would I be justified in feeling other than grateful for the glorious good all are doing?

Over lunch, my producer asked what I think about the other telecasts. I answered that if there were thousands of programs, each nationwide, each really God-directed, and each reaching people and transforming lives, there would still be room at the top for every one of them! I feel it deeply! Therefore, I pray for the other ministries as well as my own.

Victory can be yours through competition, because you are a unique person with something to offer in a way that no one else can duplicate exactly.

Welcome competition. (It's good for you!)

Pray for your competitors. (That way you share in their victories along with your own.)

Accept every opportunity to serve that you can. (Deed meeting need never goes out of style!)

Constantly improve your own service. (Service is the spirit!)

Keep open to new ideas. (Service stays fresh.)

Surround yourself with the most capable, faith-thinking helpers you can.

Go first class in your service, as much as you can.

There is plenty of room at the top for *you!*

FATIGUE

Auren Uris, writing in *Nation's Business,* makes this crystal clear. Claiming that too many of us feel 30 years old at 9 A.M. and 60 years old at 5 P.M., he says that the average worker (and may I add the average person) fatigues himself by fighting nature: "Instead of attuning himself with the natural rhythms inherent in everyone, he imposes a pattern of work that violates every cell in his body."

Is there an answer? Yes. Find your energy rhythms and work with them. This will reduce fatigue and probably get more done on a lesser outgo of energy. Here are some suggestions that will help you chart your energy periods: keep an account of the times you feel energy to burn; log the times you feel tired; mark the times you feel the sharpest mentally; record the times you find it is most difficult to work.

Uris advises us to do the hardest jobs when we have the most energy, and the easier work during low-energy periods. Take advantage of, and move with, your more natural rhythm.

SELF CONCEPT

Many people have only a foggy notion as to who they are. Others have no idea. Philosopher Arthur Schopenhauer accidentally bumped into a stranger on the street. "And just who are you?" asked the irritated stranger.

"Who am I?" replied Schopenhauer. "How I wish I knew!"

Some have lost themselves in a maze of arrogance. Life as a whole is dedicated to self. Like Mascagni, in the opera *Masks,* one lives "to myself, with distinguished esteem of unalterable satisfaction." Starting today, ask yourself some straight from the shoulder questions.

Who am I?

Where am I going?

What is my life?

What may I become?

These will take you to a depth of life where you can get
the spark of lasting tranquility. Yes, it gets to religion.
Dr. Karl Jung said that side by side with the decline of
religious life, the neuroses grow noticeably more fre-
quent. A physician assured me that, as paradoxical as it
may sound, there is nothing the matter with a nervous
person's nerves. "The ebbing of religion as an effective
force in multitudes of people has been accompanied by
an incalculable increase of nervous disorders."

The answer on which you can stake your life is outlined in these words: ". . . trust the Lord completely. . . .
In everything you do, put God first and he will direct
you and crown your efforts with success. . . . you can
sleep without fear; and you need not be afraid of disaster
or the plots of [anyone who opposes you]; for the Lord
is with you; he protects you" (Proverbs 3:5–6; 24–26,
LB).

1) God is your wonderful Friend. (You can't beat Him for
   companionship.)
2) Trust Him *completely*. (Piecemeal trust produces piecemeal peace. Maybe, that has been your trouble.)
3) Put God first in your life. (It isn't good manners to put
   royalty anywhere except on the throne!)
4) He will guide you. (And the new frontiers to which He
   will take you will probably surprise you!)
5) He will bring success to your life. (No more failures; in

everything, success—even in setbacks. If you haven't lived long enough to experience success through a setback, you haven't really lived!)

6) He will put you at ease. (For once in your life, that awful tension that has you as tight as a drum melts away in the face of your new found Power!)

7) He will help you sleep like a baby. (Tossing and turning are turned into tranquility, too!)

8) Fear will no longer defeat you. (You are afraid of neither man nor machine; the past, present, and future are enveloped by the spirit of faith!)

9) God and you live life together.

10) *Victory—victory—victory!*

All with peace for Discoverers!

LIFE-LIFTER

Substitutes subtract from life. Never settle for less than the real thing. You're worth it!

FIFTH DISCOVERY

*Live confidently and free
from tension. . . . Yes, me!*

Questions like these may gauge the depth of your confidence.

Are you friendly or hostile?

Are people attracted to you or do they shy away from you?

How do you feel when you wake up in the morning? High, low, "devil-may-care," cheerful, or grumpy?

What about an hour after you wake up? two? three? (Soon the day is gone.)

What kind of a day do you generally have? "Great!" "You-wouldn't-believe-it," or "so-so"?

How important are you making yourself to your employer? Or do you work just to live?

Are you polite or rude?

How happy is your family life?

How big are your hopes, and how tenacious are you in sticking to them?

How much of a climber in life are you? Or do you leave the peaks for the other guys (the *younger* men)?

How healthy are you? What about those migraines, nerves, tension, allergies, and ulcers? (Before you scoff this off as naïve prittle-prattle, I must tell you of a doctor who, in treating over 100 cases of arthritis and colitis, discovered that almost 70 percent were suffering from a lack of confidence, and that, in his professional judgment, this contributed significantly to their ailments!)

Are you clinging to pain and unhappiness? Perhaps unconsciously? (This is a conniving method of self-punishment encouraged by a lack of confidence.)

You may have possessed confidence in the past, but today you are drained of it. What has happened? You have allowed time to eat at it. In an effort to get across my point in a speech not long ago, I said, "Will the real *you* stand up?" Afterwards, a man high in business circles commented, "If the real Dale stood up, he'd shudder. I'm Dale," he gestured, "and I'm having a battle with what you call confidence." He told his story; it is not an uncommon one.

"I used to feel I could lick anything and everything. 'Invincible Dale' my wife called me. But the years have taken their toll. Slowly, but surely, this confidence has slipped away. Like smoke in the air."

Many people permit economic conditions, world events, reverses, old age, prospects of death, fear, and the like to pillage confidence. In fact, some people let good times ruin their confidence. When things are going well, they think something bad is bound to happen soon — which reminds me of a doctor and his new patient.

"Oh, Doctor," she exclaimed, "I have that rare and fatal disease of the liver. That new one."

The physician answered, "Nonsense. You're not suffering from that disease. As a matter of fact," he went on, "you wouldn't know whether or not you have it. That particular illness doesn't cause any discomfort whatever."

"That's the trouble," insisted the woman. "The last doctor said that. I feel better than ever! That's how I know I have it!"

You may feel out of life today. It ebbs low. Someone you deeply trusted has let you down. A friend betrayed you. A loved one has been taken from you. A mixed up world has overturned your dreams. You are out of work. Things look bleak, and you don't see much hope. There are two fearless destroyers of confidence.

DOUBT

Doubt is a wavering of opinion associated with uncertainty and instability. Doubt and *indecision* walk together. Its lifeline includes disbelief, suspicion, and fear. Doubt is a saboteur of joyous living. ". . . you must . . . not doubt at all; for whoever doubts is like a wave in the sea that is driven and blown about by the wind. Any such person must not think that he will receive anything from the Lord, for he is unsure and undecided . . ." (James 1:6–7, TEV).

How beautiful is the ocean! Sparkling sky-blue water, with white foam spliced in here and there, is rich and deep. On a trip to the Orient several years ago, I often stood on the deck of the aircraft carrier, U.S.S. *Hornet,* in between flights, and watched the gigantic swells. They heaved methodically from side to side, to and fro, as if the expansive sea were belching. Occasionally, the ocean was as placid as a kitten and as quiet as a Christmas mouse; as smooth as glass, as far as the eye could see. The ship glided through its stillness like a hot knife on butter. The swells represent the doubter's state of mind. They move. They turn and toss. But they go nowhere!

". . . driven and blown about. . . ." Exterior propulsion is the description for the doubter. Circumstances, conditions, inordinate influence by others — these lead the way for him. God has made him stand proudly on his own feet, and the Lord will provide plenty of what it takes to do that. But the doubter reneges on his God-granted position and capitulates. The doubter gives in to inferiority.

Doubt is a greedy thief of confidence, in that it destroys wonderful self-positiveness, which is God-generated. A letter I have in my files illustrates this point. After reading some of our inspirational literature, Arch M., a man in his early forties, wrote me to share his story.

Several years before, he had begun a business of his own. "It was a lifelong dream," he said. "And we had done our homework carefully, before making the big jump." The market potential was great; there was a need for his product. (Any successful venture depends a great deal on finding a need and filling it.) He developed know-how and started his company. But two years later, several bad deals set him back, and doubt moved in and began to dissipate his energies.

"I began to wonder if I had made the right move by starting my own business," he confided. "Then I started to regret it. I felt a gradual decline of confidence in the venture I had undertaken. I began to believe that I was no longer up to it. The challenge required sharp decisions, but my mind was muddled. Even my physical strength declined to a low ebb," he witnessed.

See what doubt can do? The reverses in Arch's business didn't defeat him, but doubt started to. Had he not checked it, doubt would have ruined him.

In 1965, my church, in San Dimas, California, began with a dream, a prayer, and $2,500 borrowed for publicity. Each week our dependable Falcon pulled to the drive-in theater, where our services were held: a second-hand trailer loaded with the fifteen-year-old, weather-worn Conn organ; a ten-year-old homemade pulpit; and two sprays of artificial flowers.

People, who told me that the dream of a great regional Walk-In, Drive-In Inspiration Center would never work, looked at the measly surroundings and scoffed, "I told you so." That doubt would have infected the dream, dripped dry the drive, and bombed out a work of Christ had it found a home with our people. It would have died in the thinking stage had doubt carried the day.

DOUBT REDUCES DRIVE! DOUBT RIDDLES GREAT DREAMS— KEEPS THEM AS DREAMS AND PREVENTS THEM FROM BECOMING REALITIES!

TENSION

In America, tension is almost as common as ham and eggs. The U.S. Public Health Service reports that one in five noninstitutionalized Americans has gone through a nervous breakdown or felt one coming on. Do you know what a nervous breakdown is? It's that vague term for extreme tension that brings about some degree of temporary breakup in personality.

Hypertension, a grownup brother of tension, plagues men. It's deadlier than cancer and, if you don't believe that, go out and apply for insurance, if you have it. Hypertension kills one out of four men who die after fifty years of age, claims one doctor.

This tension grows an impressive crop—peptic ulcers, muscular spasms, asthma, migraines, rheumatoid arthritis, heart trouble, and wrecked families, to mention a few. A six-year study at Columbia University, which involved disturbed children and teen-agers who were examined medically and psychiatrically, confirmed the powerful effect family tension plays in disturbances. Tension starts them and keeps them going.

Some of us function under tension, but our effectiveness is impaired. Tension leads us to the point at which the soldiers were, during the Battle of Shiloh, when General A. S. Johnston said to General Pierre Beauregard, "General, our troops are very much in the condition of a lump of sugar thoroughly soaked with water, but yet preserving its original shape, though about ready to dissolve."

How unlike the Psalmist, who, when pressured by Absalom, said, ". . . I lay down and slept in peace . . ." (3:5, LB). "I will lie down in peace . . ." (4:8, LB).

What causes our tensions? There are eight "Tension Bombs" derived from the word "T-E-N-S-E."

1) *Time.* You begin to feel that there isn't enough of it, so your system gets in a nervous hurry all over. This hurrying results in disharmony, which is enough to frighten the sensible forces out of you.

2) *Expectations.* They're so high that, even by the farthest stretch of the imagination, they are beyond reach. The superest human doesn't have a chance at them. Wild fanaticism has overruled reasonable enthusiasm. When you fail to meet them, you fall apart. An inferiority devil creeps within you and eats away. The upshot is tension. You can feel it building up.

3) *Need.* Instead of having too high expectations, you need to take the cork off your potential and move up. A sense of possibilities needles you to give fuller energies. Your problem is like that of the drowsy shoe clerks. The manager said to a customer, "So you'd like some loafers? I'll send a pair to wait on you!" Like a chick about to hatch, that drive within you is waiting to be expressed. It needs a channel. Keep it down, and tension will develop.

4) *No.* You've been unable to say a positive, gracious, definite "no," even when you knew you couldn't possibly live up to your agreement. A friend of mine had horrible migraines — blinding, nauseating, deathly headaches — until he learned to say "no," when he knew it was the right response. *The person who relinquishes himself to the mercy of too many demands will find himself manhandled and manipulated to the extent that he cannot give himself reasonably to anything or anyone.*

5) *"Nixed."* Your ideas are nixed, turned down. Dreams are thwarted. Plans are squashed. And you think the ones responsible know so much less than you. Life takes an unexpected turn. Reverse sets in; the pot within you boils and you fume bitterly. In that predicament, you're choice material for tension. What are your alternatives? *Go on with life — whether you feel like it or not.* Live with the situation and improve it — or, completely transform it.

6) *Spiritual inadequacy*. You haven't really tapped the springs. Your well is dry; send the bucket down and it comes up empty.

Dr. J. A. Hadfield (in *The Psychology of Power*) says, "Speaking as a student of psychotherapy, who, as such, has no concern with theology, I am convinced that the Christian religion is one of the most valuable and potent influences that we possess for producing that harmony and peace of mind and that confidence of soul which is needed to bring health and power to a large proportion of nervous patients."

When there is spiritual inadequacy, you haven't enough to meet the requirements of living successfully in this kind of world.

7) *Effort*. You don't know when to relax. Instead, you push yourself into collapse, forgetting that more is accomplished, and better, when you are flowing through a relaxed self. One might suspect that the staff of my congregation and the Church Board have a great deal on their hands. Each minute counts, and much needs to be done. For that reason, we limit our staff meetings to one hour and the Church Board meetings to two hours. *Fatigued people make bad decisions.*

8) *External forces*. The way of life around you — society, mechanism, computerism, numberism, the job, the government, the economy — affects you substantially. But do they control you? Do they push you around? They are exterior influences. Whatever effect exterior influences hold over you depends largely on your reaction to them.

Dr. William S. Sadler said, "I am forced to recognize that many of these [nervous disorders] are not based upon any discoverable hereditary trait. They are due largely to a vicious environment. They represent mechanism which has persistently been forced far beyond the measure of human endurance. In general, our character is destined to become what we make it by virtue of the manner in which we allow or compel ourselves to react to our environment."

For example, in an atmosphere of anger, you react angrily or with a control and poise that baffles the angered. As Tennyson said in "De Profundis," (*The Poetic & Dramatic Works of Alfred Lord Tennyson*): ". . . this main-miracle, that thou art thou / With power on thine own act and on the world."

These are some of the Tension bombs, and you must defuse them. It won't be done by trying to rid yourself of the capacity for tension.

THE MAN WHO HAS NO CAPACITY FOR TENSION HAS NO CAPACITY FOR SUCCESSFUL AND ADVENTUROUS LIVING.

Forces which, when misdirected, lead to tension are forces, which rightly directed, are behind the doers. Take a stoical approach to life and you're out of it. The completely unperturbables are breathing mummies.

Tension-ridders and confidence-builders are readily available through peace—for Discoverers.

Discoverers take each day as it comes! It may look hard; perhaps it isn't what people prefer. If they could order another one, they would, but it is the only day they have, so they take it cheerfully.

This attitude is a prime ingredient to a rewarding day, everyday. They take each day as it comes, they wake up with a meaningful feeling. "A wonderful day, God! What can I do for you today?" In this way, they learn to keep tomorrow's troubles a day away—where they belong!

Discoverers make each day as it comes. After taking it, they transform it as Mr. David Roth did.

Most people think they are out of order when they pass the age of sixty-five. A lot of them act it long before then! Arthur Godfrey said that anyone who claims he can do at fifty what he did at twenty-five didn't do much when he was twenty-five! But, at ninety-seven, Mr. Roth has a *young, alive mind.* His secret to exuberance in life is to make each day as it comes.

Discoverers settle on their purpose for living and pursue it enthusiastically. They have great resources to live from; great principles to live by; and a great purpose to live for!

Discoverers employ the more than enough principle. Rather than *just enough* to take and make the day, they have enough inside with some to spare. I urge people to use a statement that illustrates this principle:

> I am the rich child of the Heavenly Father, all that the Father has is mine. / Divine wisdom shows me how to claim these blessings. The Holy Spirit leads me in the Way. / Everything which is mine by divine inheritance now comes to me in abundance.

As the Bible says, you have more than enough strength from God's boundless resources, to have your full share of what He has for everyone of His children (Colossians 1:11–12). A man who can tell you this works is Ed T., who described himself as one of the most doubt-filled men to ever face life. A rugged, American-looking fellow, he was also one of the biggest men to ever face life— 6'7", and every ounce of 260 pounds!

But Ed trudged under the heavy load of past mistakes. They had sapped away the last strain of confidence. "I let them give me a defeatist frame of mind," he confessed. "Defeat sort of hung over me like a sinister cloud ready to unleash its fury at any minute." No man can go for long in that condition. Slowly and surely, it defunctionalized him.

One day, Ed took the advice of a business associate and began to read the Bible. Reading the Bible was a new experience for him, and he came across other verses like Colossians 1:11-12.

"Like a bolt out of the blue," Ed explained, "it occurred to me that if I owned up to the rights God offers me, I could become a confident man." When he mentioned it to another associate, whom Ed knew to be a Christian, he was told that he could begin by accepting Jesus Christ into his life.

"That threw me," Ed said. "What is 'accepting Christ'?" It was explained that "accepting Christ" means to acknowledge your need for the Lord humbly; to turn your life over to Him, receive His Spirit into your heart and mind, and begin to live Christ's way. Ed didn't find this explanation fanatical; he recognized it to be a sensible and intelligent commitment to make to God. And, being a pretty good thinker, Ed heartily and quietly responded.

"Christianity became personal," he smiled, "Ed's thing—meaningful, great!

"And, miraculously, I sensed a mastery over doubt." Since then, Ed has been living like it.

Discoverers build their confidence on the Lord! And they are never let down.

Some people confuse conceit with confidence. A man

in the hospital told me his nurse was so conceited that when she took the pulse of male patients, she allowed ten points for the impact of her personality on them!

Here is the difference: Confidence is built on character — God's, then yours. Conceit is built on clay. Under pressure it crumbles. Great people — Discoverers — build their confidence on *God!*

"The Lord is my shepherd; I shall not want." Another way to say it is, "Because the Lord is my shepherd, I have everything I need" (23:1, LB). St. Paul was so confident that he advised, ". . . be glad in the Lord" (Philippians 3:1, LB).

Even a child can realize this marvelous confidence. Tammy Scott, a sixth-grader, is one of the wonderful young friends in my life. Before Tammy's mother, Arloa, passed on to her eternal home at age thirty-nine, she had had three major operations. When Tammy got the news of the last one, she sighed, "What! Again!"

Later on that evening, after the child went to bed, her dad slipped in to tuck her in for the night. As he opened the door, he saw that Tammy had pulled the quilt over her head, and he heard her singing a hymn she had learned at church.

> God is my help in every need,
> God does my every hunger feed;
> God walks beside me, guides my way,
> Through every moment of the day.

Such confidence is one which only God can generate.

Discoverers have purpose and direction! Loss of confidence stems from loss of purpose; a directionless man is a defeated man.

I remember when I suffered a severe breakdown in confidence. How dreary the world looked! Doubt pushed me to despair. Unrest kept me on a very unpleasant spiritual edge.

"Why am I here?"

"What am I doing in the Christian ministry?"

"I'm not good enough to get the job done."

"Lord, the mission is too much for me."

At times, life can be compared to the seasons of the year, and there seems to be a winter time in life for most people. But my predicament was a raw lack of confidence. What pulled me out, or, at least, helped me greatly? A regaining of purpose for *my* life — the amazing words of Isaiah, repeated by Jesus, stimulated a new confidence in me. "The Spirit of the Lord is upon me . . . he has anointed me to preach good news. . . . He has sent me . . ." (Luke 4:18, RSV). I repeated those words dozens of times each day, until they oozed from the pores of my soul.

Get your finger on *your* purpose — why God has put *you* on this earth; why God has given *you* the opportunity to live *now* at this exact time — and glorious confidence will rise up from your heart like water from a mountain spring.

LIFE-LIFTER

Confidence results from what you are in relation to what you can become, pushed by the hardships you face — when you honestly and openly trust your life to Jesus Christ.

Marriage can really be beautiful!

Marriage may be a wonderful experience for you. Peace which gets deep enough into you to do something about your relationships is the key, because a peace that deep will bring harmony into your life and, *through you,* to your marriage experience.

On their forty-fifth anniversary, a man claimed, "I have more to be thankful for than most men with whom I've been associated down through the years. My wife is the reason. Were I to relive this day of forty-five years ago, knowing what I know now, I'd marry her again — if she'd have me! Her loving partnership has left an indelible impression on everything worthwhile I've achieved."

Obviously, those are words from a man to whom marriage has been a significant experience. It is important to develop a really meaningful relationship. Dr. Paul Popenoe, America's pioneering marriage counselor, maintains that it is the most important thing in life.

From the outset, marriage was hallowed by a sacred

beauty. ". . . a man leaves his father and his mother and cleaves to his wife, and they become one flesh" (Genesis 2:24, RSV). Jesus particularly emphasized the *unity* needed in the relationship: ". . . the two shall become one. . . . So they are no longer two but one" (Matthew 19:5–6, RSV).

We hear about the "ideal marriage." Is it one without problems? On Family Sunday, a minister said to his congregation, "Let every husband who has problems stand up." Everyone stood except one man. "Oh," exclaimed the minister, "you're one in a million." "It's not that," answered the man. "I can't stand because I'm paralyzed!"

If you are human, there are problems in your marriage. They may be small; they may be big. Never ask to have *no* problems—unless you are ready for the cemetery— ask for strength to handle the problems.

The problemless marriage is a phony relationship! No, the "ideal marriage" is *not* a problemless marriage.

Is it one in which feelings are always on cloud nine? Some couples I have counseled felt that the rose must stay in bloom the year round—their feelings had to be sky-high all the time. We admit to seasons in nature, why not allow room for seasons in feelings?

Anyone who expects his marriage to stay constantly on a high, emotional pitch will take a hard fall. Feeling down, he starts to grab at straws.

"I don't love my mate anymore."

"I can do better elsewhere."

"I know what I need—a divorce."

Such talk is marital poppycock!

Is the "ideal marriage" only a "convenient arrangement"? To get away from parents? To show you're an adult? To give a legitimate name to the baby you expect? To gain your "freedom"? To maintain your respectability? To gain way into a social set? To put you on easy street? To meet the expectations of your family? You are in for a crushing disappointment!

Then what *is* an "ideal marriage"?

It is the experience of union—a spiritual and emotional togetherness—in which two lives are being welded together daily as husband and wife. This is the unifying process—always a *process!*

There is learning, trial and error, hurt and healing, joy and sorrow in this process.

A marriage license and a spectacular wedding don't produce this process. They are but ways of declaring a beginning. What follows is infinitely more important. It is the following, however, that gets muddled. One weary man suggested that all marriages are happy. It is the living together afterwards that is tough!

The reason many marriages have no meaning in their relationship is *lack of unity.* Until the relationship begins to jell as a "oneness" of husband and wife, there will not be any measurable amount of peace in depth for either one. Unhappily married people are miserable!

There are a few exceptions, of course—men and women who live the best lives they can, in spite of trying conditions at home. Inwardly and individually, they manage to achieve a measure of compatibility when a marital storm rages around them. To these tremendous souls, we tip our hat. Yet, how much more life would mean to them if they had emotional and spiritual oneness with their partner.

How can you realize a more honest to goodness unity in your marriage?

8 STEPS TO THE MARRIAGE RELATIONSHIP
YOU WANT

Talk!

Use realistic communication. Someone has described a monologue as a conversation between husband and wife. One man in California answered a police complaint that he and his wife had some words. "I had some," he said, "but I didn't get a chance to use them."

Words represent you! More often than not, what you say tells what you are. A person talks madly because he is mad within. Communication expresses it. Therefore, when husband and wife talk, they are opening up "them" to each other.

David and Joyce Ireland of Arcadia, California, believe that honest talk is the basis of their happy marriage. David, a marriage counselor, is also a quadraplegic. The victim of a rare neurological disease, he says, "I feel in my own soul that I have a lot to give in life. I don't feel my own physical problems should limit what I have to give." Both Irelands admit that they have had to work at communication; it didn't come naturally. It doesn't to most people!

I have in my files "A Blueprint for Successful Marriage," from the Conciliation Court of the Los Angeles County Superior Court. It reads:

Without good communication between a husband and wife, the marriage relationship begins to suffer from great pressures and tensions. Communication is as vital to a marriage as oxygen is to the human body. Good communication is a skill which can be developed with practice.

It seems strange that two people can live under the same roof, joined together in life's most intimate relationship, and yet find it difficult, if not impossible, to discuss problems vitally affecting their marriage and children. Yet all too frequently such is the case. This is called an "inability to communicate."

Many reasons can be responsible for this verbal barrier between husband and wife. Pride, guilt, embarrassment, loss of self-confidence or inexperience in frankly expressing one's personal feelings are some causes for the condition.

The end result often is misunderstanding, frustration, and anger, the home filled with tension and unhappiness. The marriage partners develop feelings of isolation and rejection. The unfulfilled yearnings they have for each other become a gnawing hunger.

Lacking communication the marriage is left without an emotional safety valve. Too often hidden resentments are taken out on minor children, thereby increasing the turmoil in the home.

This communication link is a skill which can be developed with practice. Seven rules to follow are:

1) Select a time when you are less tense and free from pressures of the day.
2) In a friendly way, invite your partner to a conference.
3) Keep the conference private — no kids, please!
4) Consider openly your partner's points of view.
5) Avoid arguments and quarrels. Mutually agree to adjourn the conference if they should start.
6) Share — communication is a *two*-way street.
7) Keep two very reliable words available: "I'm sorry."

Excuse!

Forgive! You and your marriage are too important to be spoiled by bitterness. You are too valuable to hold resentments and grudges. One of the most wonderful memories I hold is of an amazing wife, whose husband walked out on her with another woman after nineteen years of marriage. During the next two years, this woman discovered several answers that renewed the couple and got them started on a mature relationship. But, without her forgiveness, none of the steps would have worked.

In the absence of forgiveness, resentment builds up. It is a spiritual containment which imprisons life, paralyzes life, blinds life, and may even terminate life. It produces a sullen malice and ingrown crankiness that makes one unfit to be around. It is harbored ill will, and any sensible person recognizes that is a sorry way to face life, the day, oneself, and others.

The honest thing to do is to put injuries aside and go on with life. By nursing resentment along, we keep alive something that will kill us. It dulls the sharp edge a marriage may have. It dims the fun in a marriage relationship.

A heartbroken man in Arizona wrote me, "After twenty-two years of marriage, it looks like ours is coming to an end. Ann has decided she loves a man young enough to be her son. She has asked me for a divorce. I'm in such a predicament! For the past few months, everything seems wrong. I see no way out."

I prayed about an answer for him. The clearest impression I received was to help him beat resentment. If it didn't save his marriage, at least, it would save him. I wrote him about it. Several months went by before I received another letter. The marriage ended in divorce, but he was spared from an embittered spirit.

Before you begin to feel that anybody in your circumstances would feel resentful, let me tell you of young Jim Mackey. If bitterness is ever legitimate, Jim had a right to feel that way.

At fourteen, he was a great little athlete—full of life and vitality. The townsfolk had already pegged him for really big things. But one day, Jim began to limp. No one paid much attention to it at first, but, when the pain didn't go away, he was taken to the doctor.

Jim had cancer, and his leg had to be amputated. Before long, though, he was back at school hobbling around on crutches.

"Soon I'll have my wooden leg. And, guys," he cheerfully boasted, "I'll be able to hold up my socks with a thumbtack! How's that for class! Betcha none of you can do it!"

When football season started, Jim asked if he could be a team manager. Of course they were pleased to have a spunky fellow like Jim around; a person like that does something for you. Then, one day, Jim missed practice. He was at the doctor's office again. The examination showed that he had lung cancer. "He'll be dead in six weeks," the physician predicted. Jim's parents told him about it, so he could make the most of those six weeks.

Jim returned to school and his team. Again, he spread his buoyant faith and determination all around. The team had an undefeated season. As a fitting climax, the boys decided to have a big banquet in honor of their magnificent team manager, Jim Mackey. At the banquet, they planned to present him with a team football, autographed by each member of the squad. But Jim was unable to attend because of his illness.

A few weeks later, he was back in school, rather gaunt and sickly-looking. Still, he had that precious humor, bright outlook and winsome spirit.

"Jim," said the coach softly, "where have you been? We had a banquet just for you, you know."

"Aw, coach," Jim smiled, "you know I'm on a diet. Doctor's orders!"

One of the boys walked up to hand him the team football. "We won because of you, big man," his teammate said. "From all of us with a big thanks." As Jim accepted the ball, a few tears trickled down his tightly-drawn cheeks.

He turned around to leave.

"Coach," he said as he reached the door, "It's goodbye this time. I'm ready."

Two days later, Jim passed on.

Resentment didn't get to him. Victory! Victory! Victory!

Success of this nature can be yours in your marriage if you *excuse!* In the marriage relationship, forgiveness has three very distinctive characteristics:

1) Accept your partner as he is. (If you are unwilling to take your partner as he is before marriage, you had better not take him at all!)
2) Help him become the person he can be. (Example, not coercion, please!)
3) Accept him *now;* help him now. Help yourself to help him.

Adjust!

Marriage is a relationship where the most give and take is necessary. At the root of most marriage problems is selfishness.

The *"I take"* attitude prevails over the *"I give"* attitude. Naturally, the health of your relationship depends both on giving and receiving. If you do not receive, soon you will have nothing to give. When you stop receiving, it is only a matter of time until you are unable to give. If you do not give, you will become stagnant, and your source will dry up.

In every successful marriage, there is adjustment — not just a single shot of it; but a continuing, growing life of it. One of the most effective ways of developing this healthy, giving relationship is to remind yourself, at least once a week, just how much your partner has to take from you in order to maintain a happy relationship.

Meet!

Your husband or wife has needs. Everyone does! Here are ten needs of a marriage partner.

APPEARANCE A wife who looks her best excites her husband. The husband who maintains a fine appearance keeps his wife interested. But, as years roll by, people often let themselves look like slouches.

"A Blueprint for Successful Marriage" states:

> During the years when persons are courting one another, and generally speaking for a few years thereafter, each is very careful about his own personal appearance. However, as time goes on, all too frequently a husband and wife tend to take each other for granted and assume that the love of one for the other is permanent. As a result, quite often one or the other allows his personal appearance to take a very secondary place to the other cares and responsibilities of married life.
>
> Such things as uncleanliness, overweight, vulgarity, or carelessness in dress, can become repulsive and offensive to the other party.

You make a costly mistake when you underestimate the power of appearance!

APPRECIATION It instills a sense of worth, but it, too, falls by the side as a marriage casualty when routine takes over. *In How to Help Your Husband,* Mrs. Dale Carnegie said:

> Some of us don't realize how many small services our husbands do for us every day, just because we are so used to having these tasks done for us. My husband once seemed to me to be the helpless type who couldn't get a drink of water without making it a major operation. He couldn't change the baby's diapers or fix a leaky tap. Yet, when he was away in Europe one summer, I was amazed to find how many chores he had been doing for me every day—without a word of thanks—which I now had to do for myself!

COMMUNITY *His* and *hers* may cause great difficulty in a marriage. *Ours* is a wonderful word and a requirement for the successful relationship you deserve.

COMPENSATION You have weaknesses; your partner does, too. Each must compensate for the other's shortcomings. When your husband or wife is:

angry, be temperate;

sad, be glad;

dejected, be courageous;

quarrelsome, be sensible;

troubled, be peaceful;

cutting and sarcastic, be gentle and kind;

hateful, be helpful and understanding;

faithless, be faith-filled.

What may happen? The corresponding attitude and feeling tends to be created in your partner. This is the

Law of Identical Transference, often evidenced in Jesus' life.

COMPLIMENTS They are like little flowers that beautify the way. Counseling a troubled couple, I asked if the husband ever gave her a compliment. "Well," she answered, "sometimes he says, 'If you're not a nice one!'" Another wife explained, "He never notices when I look great. But let me look bad and he has a lot to say!"

Spoken sincerely, compliments will bring your partner to life!

COURTESY Be as polite to each other as to your best friends. That is a rule that will never fail you.

FUNDS Share spending money! Not only is it fair, it makes reasonable freedom possible. I've known men who hand out dimes to their wives as they do to a beggar. This attitude builds a ridiculous dependence problem, and it damages one's sense of personal respect. The wife feels like a leech.

PERSONHOOD Your partner must maintain the liberty to develop as a person. Some have felt that marriage vows restrict personal growth. This is wrong! It doesn't, and it must never be allowed to.

When you have interests that differ, make room for personhood. As Dr. Paul Popenoe says, "Partners may have different interests, but they must be basically sympathetic toward each other" (*Los Angeles Times,* September 17, 1968). The famous counselor adds that one must have sympathy with each other's aims and interests.

PROMPTNESS If you haven't got it, now is the time to begin to develop a sense of time. Your mate needs it. You have no more right to keep your husband or wife waiting, than you do the purchasing agent in a million-dollar sale.

Couples in Los Angeles are assured in the *Times* article that it is important not to maintain late and unusual hours or to stay away from home without advising the other of this necessity in advance, and of the place where such party may be reached in the event of emergencies.

SEXUALITY As an expression of love, sex is the most beautiful, fulfilling experience a couple may have. Love is an emotion that transcends all other feelings; consequently, in filling your partner's need, you may have to participate in a sexual experience, occasionally, when you don't feel like it. Of course, reasonableness must play its positive role.

You must help meet those needs—another way of saying, "Care." After years of study and on-the-job observation, Dr. Manfred Hecht of New York felt that every husband and wife needs emotional support and to feel they belong. Respect, understanding, kindness, honesty, optimism, realism, tidiness, and recognition — these are the deepest needs human beings have. Four ways you may meet your partner's needs:

Be sensitive to one another's needs. (Feel for one another! Feel with one another!)

Be receptive to each other. (Don't reject or ignore your partner. OK, you may have to go out of your way and put down your "I don't want to" feelings occasionally!)

Be ready to listen. (Attentiveness!)

Accept differences that prove to be unresolvable. (You don't have to be perfect! Neither does your partner!)

In *The Master Key to Riches,* Napoleon Hill states that the real riches of life increase in exact proportion to the scope and extent of the benefit they bring to those with whom they are shared. Nowhere is this truer than in the marriage relationship!

Love!

Love is really the heart of a successful marriage — that is, a growing and maturing love. A couple can take anything, stand anything, and go through anything when there is honest love for each other. The big trouble is mushy feelings — sentiment instead of a deep affection; starry eyes rather than an abiding admiration. Many couples have gone no farther than ankle deep in their relationship. Others have lost their love. It has been choked out!

The couple that came by my office to see me one day had almost everything going for them. "We're probably the most successful mess you've seen," they greeted me. In their mid-thirties, with three fine children, they headed a growing advertising business, lived in a $50,000 home, and watched their bank account get fatter and fatter. But their marriage was breaking apart! Oh, yes, they were honorable enough to keep it together until the children got off to college — one of those twenty-plus years' divorces!

"What's the trouble?" I asked.

Their answer is as familiar as the hills: "We don't love each other."

"Did you ever love one another?"

"Yes, years ago. But slowly, it has died out."

They let it die out, but the flame can be revived. They

retrieved their love. Although it had been reduced to ashes, it responded to positive effort.

Marriage unity is built around love, romanticism included. Fan the embers and you will be surprised at the turn upward in your relationship!

At all weddings, I mention the *Key to a Really Successful Marriage* relationship. It is a paraphrase of I Corinthians 13:4–8 (PHILLIPS).

> This love of which I speak is slow to lose patience — it looks for a way of being constructive. It is not possessive; it is neither anxious to impress nor does it cherish inflated ideas of its own importance.
>
> Love has good manners and does not pursue selfish advantage. It is not touchy. It does not compile statistics of evil or gloat over the wickedness of other people (including your partner!). On the contrary, it is glad with all good men when Truth prevails.
>
> Love knows no limit to its endurance, no end to its trust, no fading of its hope; it can outlast anything. It is, in fact, the one thing that still stands when all else has fallen.

Remember, a healthy marriage demands that you fall in love *many* times — with the same person!

Integrity!

Integrity is the stuff *you,* as a person, are made of. When you are true to yourself, you can be true to your husband or wife. And when you are with yourself in the night hours, the mirror of your mind will reflect thankfulness, appreciation, and self-respect. Integrity is the only way to an honest marriage relationship. The secret lies as much in becoming the "right" person as it does in finding the right partner.

Faith!

Faith in one another is a wonderful thing. It is a sustaining force even if everything else is lost. Money can be lost. Cars can be lost. Houses can be lost. Associates can be lost. Jobs can be lost. But faith—faith, when it is kept, keeps you going. Keep it up and it will keep you up. I have known couples who got to the point where faith was the only thing between them and oblivion. *Faith is also a place to begin again,* for it is a confident attitude of expectancy.

"Life will work out!"

"Our marriage will be better!"

"Let's give it another try!"

Enthusiasm!

Without enthusiasm, the marriage relationship is incomplete. The fire is out. As Henry David Thoreau said, "None are so old as those who have outlived their enthusiasm."

Enthusiasm in your marriage will make it spurt ahead to a more unifying relationship. It will bring zest and life to the relationship.

Combine these eight elements and you will begin an ideal marriage—not a marriage in which two people marry to be happy, but one to make each other happy and, thereby, to derive ultimate personal happiness.

In this chapter, I have shared eight words: *talk, excuse, adjust, meet, love, integrity, faith,* and *enthusiasm.* Take the first letter of each word and put them together, and they spell *team life!*

MARRIAGE IS A TEAM LIFE, A TEAM RELATIONSHIP, A TEAM
EXPERIENCE!

The complete team has not two, but three members —
husband, wife, and Christ.

As the words of one marriage liturgy says, "The ever-
living Christ is here to bless you. The nearer you keep
to Him, the nearer you will be to one another."

His Presence brings about a change *in* you. Then the
emphasis shifts to *being* the right person more than
finding or making the right person of the other.

Earlier, I mentioned the wife whose husband left her
after nineteen years of marriage. The road to reconcilia-
tion began when she volunteered a prayer of promise.
"Dear Lord, my marriage is a mess. I can't solve it. You
can! I'll do anything You tell me. And I'll wait as long
as You tell me to wait. Thank You. Amen."

Months, tears, work, and changes later, her Team
Member — Christ — became *their* Team Member. In His
love and strength, they are building a happy marriage.
The family is discovering completeness and wholeness.
Peace is doing wonders in them!

LIFE-LIFTER

Marriage is too wonderful to be wrecked, or to make a
wreck out of you. The relationship you need will not be
achieved in a single day. It is a process and it takes
strivers.

SEVENTH DISCOVERY

Release the power to reach the stars

Perhaps you have not fully realized that there are stars for *you*, specifically set out for *you* and within *your* reach! They are areas of achievement for which you are suited, or can be. Your stars may be unlike those set out for other people. What about vocations? One person may be better suited to become a teacher, someone else a businessman.

I know two brothers, one of whom is a physician, while the other is an attorney. Why aren't both of them doctors or lawyers? Because each has his own star. Al is a great attorney; that is his inclination. Frank is a tremendous surgeon; that is the best use of his abilities.

You have stars, too, and in your conscious and subconscious self, you yearn for strength to reach them. You feel you need to:

HAVE MORE CONFIDENCE IN YOURSELF.

OVERCOME THAT DEFEATING LOW SELF-ESTEEM.

TRY THAT NEW IDEA.

PROPOSE SOME IMAGINATIVE ACTION YOU FEEL IS NEEDED.

DREAM BIGGER AND PRAY DEEPER.

BE SURER OF YOURSELF.

MEET PROBLEMS WITHOUT COMING UNRAVELED.

HANDLE PROBLEMS SUCCESSFULLY.

BECOME A BETTER FRIEND.

SURROUND YOURSELF WITH TRUE FRIENDS.

HAVE A DYNAMIC ATTITUDE.

HAVE ASSURANCE THAT THE GRAVE ISN'T THE END.

HAVE ASSURANCE THAT YOUR LOVED ONES LIVE ON.

Fulfillment of all these needs is within your reach. The secret is *released power*. The principle of released power is more than a self-generation of power. It is power *released* through you. It doesn't need to be drummed up. You are unable to produce it, for, humanly speaking, it is far beyond you. Why should you? This power is already there and available!

You don't need to manufacture electricity to light your house; it is made and ready for use. You simply release it by flipping the switch. The simplest, yet most dynamic, far-reaching, life-changing, light-shedding truth about life that I can mention is that *power* is there — take it!

GREAT ACHIEVEMENTS DEPEND ON
RELEASED POWER!

Handel's *Messiah* is a masterpiece. I hear it at least once each year and each time goose pimples pop out all over me. It is recognized by most experts as the greatest oratorio ever produced. Written in an unbelievably short twenty-four days, Handel was inspired from the outset of its composition.

He was under an uninterrupted spell. When he completed the breathtaking "Hallelujah Chorus," Handel told a companion that he thought he had seen all of heaven before him, and the great God Himself. And, after the entire piece was finished, he confided to a physician that he thought God had visited him.

Handel didn't conjure the power, did he? He released it! He was an instrument through which it flowed. He was a vehicle!

Fragile and human as they are, ministers feel this way, at times. A message comes through the preacher — falling like embers of fire from his lips, lighting and electrifying his listeners, moving them to peaks of Christian experience and motivating them to positive action. I credit it to the flow of *power;* for the Spirit of the Lord is upon the man, anointing him to bring the good news. The man isn't concocting it; he is releasing it. This unusual inspiration, however, is not exclusively for ministers. It is available to you.

RELEASED POWER IS A DEEP NEED

Dr. Alfred Adler, the noted psychiatrist, said that our will-to-power is central and controlling. That is true whether you are fifteen or fifty, despite what Gene Barry says about middle age. "It's that period of life when you're still able to do as much as ever, but you'd rather not." Release the power! Release it and you'll reach your stars at any age! Your will-to-power will have backbone to it and substance in it. Thereby, your life: *donates instead of demands; contributes rather than contrives; relays more than receives.*

Through you flow streams of tingling water. The source is higher, fuller, richer than mere humans — and inexhaustible!

RELEASED POWER PRODUCES PRACTICAL RESULTS

Someone sent a college student my book, *Peace Through a New You.* "The most amazing thing has happened," he told me. "I must share it with you." He said that his family wasn't college-conscious and that he was the first one to go beyond the tenth grade. "They haven't discouraged me, but they haven't encouraged me either," he explained. As you might expect, he had some reservations when he entered college, but he was willing to try. Three weeks before his first big exam, he began to worry. "I couldn't get any relief. There was an awful foreboding about me. I felt the pressure."

Then he began to read *Peace Through a New You.* (Although this specific chapter isn't in that edition, the idea of released power is there.)

"It dawned on me," he claims, "that there was power available to bring me some peaceful thinking. I read the six chapters through six times." (That is enough to do something, I am positive!) Well, he let the power flow — the power of Christ. It touched his feelings, his thoughts, his muscles, his nerves, his tissues, his cells, his ligaments, his bones — "everything about me," he smiled. "And my worry took a vacation." As for the tests, he surprised himself by how well he did!

RELEASED POWER PUTS A NEW LIFE AT YOUR FINGERTIPS

Wherever you have been with your life up to now, a new day awaits you through released power. Eye has not seen nor ear heard what God has prepared for you when released power gets hold of you. What you have dreamed for is possible through released power.

Discoverer's Peace Does It!

When you are operating with peace in the depths, there is no limit to what you can accomplish, and the joy you may experience.

After his retirement, former boxing champion Archie Moore gave himself to the fight for mind ecology. He called himself "a sort of social ecologist." He has a lot on his hands, for, when a person gets the mental pollutants out and a peaceful outlook in, he is a new individual with new hopes and dreams. He is on his way up because he is on the way within.

Founder of the ABC Clubs — "Any Boy Can" — Moore challenges young people, expecially blacks, to break out of their personally imposed shells and move ahead, through more self-confidence, pride, and appreciation for school. This is a good way to crack the pressed-down barrier.

You will discover that peace makes each day a profitable day. Since your thinking in the morning does much to set the pattern for the day, a peaceful mental outlook prepares you for it by bringing hopeful, cheerful, and vital thoughts. Panic thoughts make the day nervous and fidgety; negative thoughts make it dull and wasteful. But, with Discoverer's peace, you will function rapidly and more effectively, for there is *peace* within. You become a *performer—positive, practical, pleasing, passing, and perdurable.*

There is a mighty force behind you. St. Paul spoke of it: "To him who is able to do so much more than we can ever ask for, or even think of, by means of the power working in us . . ." (Ephesians 3:20, TEV).

Discoverer's Peace Gets You to Believe Enough!

What power is released! One of the incidents from the life of Jesus that means a great deal to me concerns the father who brought his agony-ridden, convulsive, mentally-fraught, pitiful son to the Master. Please look on him in mercy, the father asked, as he watched his boy roll in a fitful spectacle on the ground. If you can, do something! Christ replied, "If I can?" "If you believe, anything is possible!" Not knowing if his faith were enough, the father answered that he did believe, but "help me to have more!"

When do you believe enough to release this power?

Must you be an expert?

Must you have all the answers?

Must you be an angel?

Does everything have to be going your way?

Must the flowers be in full bloom?

Or snow on the ground?

Must you be old?

or young?

or a certain color?

or of certain means?

or tall, short, slim, or fat?

Must you be able to account for a surefire, calculated result?

Hugh Allen reminds us that people are not like rockets and should accept the fact that seldom, if ever, in a man's life are all systems go.

Then, how much is enough? Enough to trust God! And enough to get going! At such a time, waiting makes you like the old gentleman who, before he would cross, sat by the river until all the water ran out. *What you can do, or dream you can do, with God's help, begin!* Starting has courage, genius, and power in it. Start, and your mind heats up. More spiritual power will come to you. Ways and means unfold. Believing enough says,

SOMETHING GOOD IS GOING TO HAPPEN!

PLUCK, NOT LUCK, MAKES THE DIFFERENCE!

Discoverer's Peace Gives Try-Again Power!

Remember the young lawyer from Springfield? Abe Lincoln ran for the legislature and lost; then a business venture flopped. The girl he loved dearly died. In 1846, he tried politics again, and he was elected to the Congress, served a term, and went down in a bid for reelection. He sought an appointment to the United States

Land Office and was rejected. "Doesn't a man ever learn?" friends thought. "Abe," someone must have said confidentially, "between you and me, it's time for you to settle down and make something out of yourself."

He listened, then promptly entered the race for United States Senator and was thoroughly trounced. In 1856, he was a candidate for the vice-presidential nomination. You guessed it—he lost! People looked at Lincoln and saw *"loser"* written across his life. (The crowd at the cross looked at Jesus Christ and wagged their heads over a loser; a has-been; a hopeless case!) But 1860 was a different story! Abraham Lincoln became *President of the United States of America!*

Incredible!

Unbelievable!

He wasn't "unbobbleable," but he *was* unsinkable. Lincoln had the resilient spirit everyone needs. Otherwise, you will not withstand the shocks and shoves life surely brings. Hence, there will be a rupture in your life—perhaps a deformation of spirit.

What can you count on?

There is a crown beyond your cross.

The cross often is the way to the crown.

The cross may well prepare you for the crown.

The cross adds meaning—real significance—to the crown.

Therefore, when you fall, waste no time in getting back up. "When I fall, I rise" (Micah 7:8, MOFFATT). But get up right when you get right up. No matter how many times you fall, never quit trying when what you are trying is good and God is leading you. God cares for you when times are hard, and if you fall, it isn't fatal (Psalms 37:19, 24, LB). If you aren't sure whether it is worth another try, ask questions like these:

Is God in it?

Is it helpful for others?

Does it really utilize my possibilities?

Is it the best use of me?

Can it stand adversity?

God has brought the Valley Community Church in San Dimas, California, a long way since its first Easter service at a drive-in theater in 1965. Now, you may hear stirring music from the Chancel Choir and Ensemble on Sundays. But we have a choir only because we tried again.

"Why not start a choir?" someone suggested. That lit the fuse! Dreams for a great choir were big. Hopes were high. The evening was set for the initial meeting, and it was at our place. Mrs. Ray cleaned the house until it sparkled. She baked a heaping platter of cookies and made a big pot of fresh coffee. "Got to have some refreshments for a gathering of this kind," she remarked.

At 7:30 we stood behind a closed door ready to fling it open to the surging, rushing, clamoring, enthusiastic crowd of eager singers. Surprise! Surprise! No one showed up! (I ate leftover cookies for a long time, but eventually, the coffee hardened and had to be thrown away.)

Six months later, we tried again. A few people came — a very few — so few that it reminded me of the worship service an anxious old maid attended. The crowd was so small that the eligible minister was afraid to address them as "Dearly Beloved" for fear she would take it personally! But you don't have to have a big crowd to begin. An idea, God, faith, and a willingness to put everything else you've got into it — that is sufficient. So, we had the beginnings of the Chancel Choir. *Try again* is a solid winner!

Discoverer's Peace Hangs On!

You may reach the point where you wonder:

Is there meaning to life?

What does *my* life mean?

Does my life mean anything?

What is my source in an emergency?

What is essential for living?

Can I have what I actually need?

How?

Abraham Lincoln made his crises into a schoolroom. One lesson that came to him still blesses men: "When you come to the end of your rope, tie a knot in it and hang on."

One day as I stood beside the hospital bed of a twice-widowed, fortyish, church member, she said, "I really don't care if I don't get well. Is that an awful thing to say? I feel that I'm losing my faith, and I don't want to face another tragedy. What can you tell a person like me, Reverend?"

I share these two words: "Hang on." I assured her that God would see her through, because He saw Christ through a cross and a grave. "Hang on," I said. And I guaranteed her that hundreds of vibrant Christians would help her hang on. "We'll not let you stay down."

Aldous Huxley had his hands on a truth when he said that experience is not what happens to you. It is what you do with what happens to you.

Christ turned

A trap into a triumph.

Thorns into a temple.

Darkness into dancing.

Night into noon.

Tears into a tonic.

A tomb into thanksgiving.

Death into depth.

You will discover the power a soldier left when he was blown to bits. A young companion who saw him fall said, "It'll take more than that to stop you."

The Gift from Discoverer's Peace Is the I-Can Spirit!

Thomas Carlyle, Scotland's favorite historian and essayist, challenged, "Put forth thy hand in God's name. Know that the word 'impossible' where truth and mercy and the everlasting voices of nature order, has no place in the brave man's dictionary." David of old surely felt this when he went out to meet the Philistine giant. He had the I-can spirit. "The Lord will put you into my power this day. . . . All those who are gathered here shall see that the Lord saves neither by sword nor spear" (1 Samuel 17:46, 47, NEB). With God who gives the peace and produces Discoverers out of people, anyone — you, too, yes, *you!* — can go to the stars, *your* stars!

LIFE-LIFTER

Power is available to you to LIVE forever — a day at a time, and to win in every struggle — a step at a time!

EIGHTH DISCOVERY

My misfortune can be fortunate

In this modern age, are intelligent people to suppose that misfortune can ever be fortunate? No doubt, you know what is meant by "misfortune." You have gone through it. The truth is, many people miss a fortune on misfortune, because they see misfortune only as an unfortunate development.

Never mope over a setback. Move ahead from it! At the age of ninety-five, with enthusiasm and principles undimmed, J. C. Penney thrived on the motto "beat yesterday." In some sixty-eight years, he pyramided a mining community shop to 1,700 retail stores — not, however, without some misfortunes. He credits his success to the application of the Golden Rule.

When Penney bought his butcher shop in Longmont, Colorado, his health and pocketbook were already badly broken from trying to pay off debts in Missouri. But the still young J. C. could not be kept down. He was told that in order to keep the business of the town's leading hotel, he had to give the chef a bottle of choice bourbon every week.

He delivered the first bottle, but it was against his principles, and he reflected at length on some of the values instilled in him by his father: *Never resort to an expediency; never compromise with a wrong.*

As a result, he refused to follow up with the weekly oblation to the chef, promptly lost the hotel business, and went broke. Yet, he was a winner and he knew it!

He managed to borrow $2,000 to open a drygoods store in Wyoming, and that was the beginning of his present empire.

A study of great people shows misfortunes of all kinds in their lives. John Bunyan was in jail when he wrote the immortal *Pilgrim's Progress.* Beethoven, whose music has charmed troubled souls for 200 years, never heard his majestic pieces — he was deaf! John Milton, who penned *Paradise Lost* and *Paradise Regained,* was blind. Joseph, sold into slavery, became Egypt's prime minister. Paul, the Apostle with an "obligation to all people," had his "thorn in the flesh."

The best guess is that he was slowly going blind. But we don't know exactly what the problem was, since Paul mentioned the limitation only once, and he did not identify it. Imagine that! Half of the books in the New Testament were written by Paul, yet he never described the big misfortune of his life. Not even once! How unlike many of us!

Quickly and often we refer to our limitations, centering a whole conversation around them!

"Oh, you know, I had a terrible operation. It was ghastly. The pain was really unbearable, let me tell you! See the scars.

"You don't see them? . . . Get closer.

"There, see them now? Isn't this one a beaut? I almost

died, you know." And on, and on, and on like a stuck record.

What happened the last time you went through some rugged moments? Did they throw you? Tumble you? Confuse you? Toss you into a tizzy? Squash you into a quandary? Many people are inclined to submit a resignation to tough times.

If you resign to hardships, don't be surprised when they accept the resignation, then crush you! I am convinced that misfortune may:

> Show depth of soul, for the challenge is not there to weaken you, but to strengthen you;

> Offer a fuller dimension to your life;

> Purify your life;

> Introduce you to your deeper, real self;

> Introduce you to God.

Bill Sands discovered these facts, while he was in San Quentin Prison. When he went into the penitentiary, Bill was sure the end of the world had come. His life was ruined, forever marred, and certainly marked. But something wonderful happened there! Bill got his heart and his thinking straightened out. Warden Clinton Duffy said that the change was amazing!

The prison experience woke Bill up! It induced a receptivity to the higher ways of life! It stimulated his possibilities. After his release, he began to work with prisoners. Out of the thousands of men for whom he has personally cared, 90 percent are living good lives today. They have become contributors to the communities in which they live.

Sometimes it takes a boot on the backside to get us going! When a person is flat on his back, there is only one way to look—up! A challenge can have that positive effect—sort of a shock treatment.

A young woman was dying. But the root of her trouble was that she didn't have the will to live. "I'm going to die," she kept saying, perhaps relishing the attention being heaped on her. The doctor toiled futilely, but nothing seemed to help.

"I've got an idea" the husband told the doctor. They agreed on it, so the husband walked over to her bed and said, "Liz, it looks like you're really a goner. I have to accept it, and I'll miss you very much. I think when you're gone, I'll marry Agnes." Agnes was the flame of his bachelor days—Liz's enthusiastic rival! As if stuck by a pin, Liz leaped straight up in her "death bed" and shouted, "Oh, no you won't, little boy!" From that time on, she began to improve. She was jolted back into life, got well, and is living today.

Many of our misfortunes are self-generated. You may be having financial problems because of little or no planning. Or you may have marital problems because you haven't given the care to your marriage you should. You may be playing around with your secretary, your boss, your neighbor, or your old friend. You may have serious emotional upsets because you are scared inside. Life is frightening. Depression swamps you. Bad news demolishes you. You are stymied by a fear neurosis and it has practically brought life to a standstill.

An emergency can become a crown instead of a calamity—a chance instead of a casket! Obstacles pop up inevitably, in everyone's life. They may dim you or dedicate you to the opportunities before you.

Samuel G. Howe was a great American. His motto, engraved at the Massachusetts School for the Blind, shows the magnanimous spirit he possessed: "Obstacles are things to be overcome."

For most people, their accomplishments are directly proportionate to the adversities they must surmount! As a boy in North Carolina, Lee Braxton was hopelessly bound to poverty. Lee was the tenth of twelve children. It was a struggle for him to get through the sixth grade, which ended his formal education. As a lad, Lee made out for himself. He shined shoes, sold newspapers, delivered groceries, worked in a mill, washed cars, and helped as a mechanic. Finally, he moved up to shop foreman. Things looked rather bright for the country boy.

Then, he lost his job and the house he had toiled so faithfully to get. Everything went down with one exception—*Lee Braxton!* He took command of his adversities!

On the strength of his faith and undying spirit, Lee made a new start. In time, he organized the First National Bank and became its first president. He built a hotel and started a financing company to carry the new cars sold through his automobile agency. To tend to their upkeep, he became an automobile parts dealer. He was involved in many other enterprises also—like a music company, forty-six corporations for which he served as a director, and his terms as one of the great mayors in the state.

But, at the age of forty-four, Lee put his business interests in trust and began to give his full time and abilities to religious causes. For the past twenty years, he has been the business brain and chief fund raiser behind one of America's leading ministers.

When you allow adversity to hide, blur, decrease, or

decay opportunities, it's time to believe again: "I can do all things through Christ which strengtheneth me" (Philippians 4:13, KJV).

From my own experience, I have found out that:

Setbacks can be powerful teachers.

Failure is never fatal unless you agree to it.

Success is never final.

A hard fall can lead to a high bounce.

Every adversity has an advantage.

Each loss has a corresponding gain.

Loss is temporary, if you insist on it.

Tough challenges lead to fantastic achievements.

Very few people go straight through to victory without momentary delays and temporary setbacks.

TAKE MISFORTUNE AND MAKE THE MOST OF IT FOR LIFE!

Over 100 years ago, a French citizen left a large sum of money to the French Academy to furnish prizes to Frenchmen selected on the basis of their public display of virtue and bravery. Jeanne Chaix was the oldest of six children; her mother was insane, and her father chronically sick. That left Jeanne the only one to bring up an entire family. She worked in a pasteboard factory for pittance wages, which she used to maintain the household.

The French Academy records state that Jeanne "subsisted, morally as well as materially, by the sole force of her valiant will." So did her family, the members of which drew constantly from her courage and stamina. She could have become embittered by life—it had been tough on her. But she stood there to receive the French Academy award with a smile in her heart and a radiance on her face that lit up those distinguished chambers.

Neither despise nor resent the reverses! *If you dig into them, you will discover some amazing new possibilities!*

BREAK FREE BY LOOKING AT THE MISFORTUNE AS A NEW OPPORTUNITY!

To the defeatist, "o" is the end of zero. To the winner, "o" is the beginning of opportunity. I recall when it was Darla's turn to lead our family in prayers. (We encourage the children to talk to God in their own way, so, for the first time in her life, eight-year-old Darla began a spontaneous prayer.)

She coughed up some pretty heavy words for her: "relatives," "apparently,"—words we didn't know were in her vocabulary. Then she prayed, "Thank you, God, for this op-por-tun-ity. . . ." She stopped. I thought she had probably paused to collect her thoughts and breath, so I kept my eyes closed. There was absolute silence for quite a while. Then, her twelve-year-old brother's curiosity got the best of him; he looked over at her questioningly. Then Darla whispered to him, "I don't even know what that means!"

Possibly *you* didn't know that a misfortune may be a wonderful opportunity. The word "opportunity" comes from the old days when a ship had to wait for the tide before it could make port. *Ob* plus *portus* means standing over near the port until high tide. Shakespeare felt he expressed the meaning of it when he wrote these lines for Brutus in *Julius Caesar:*

> There is a tide in the affairs of men,
> Which, taken at the flood, leads on to fortune;
> Omitted, all the voyage of their life
> Is bound in shallows and in miseries.
> On such a full sea are we now afloat;
> And we must take the current when it serves,
> Or lose our ventures.

ACCEPT YOUR SITUATION OR CHANGE IT

Convert minuses into plusses and defeats into projects. Dr. Alfred Adler, the famous psychiatrist, claims that one of the most wonderful things about human beings is their capacity to turn reverses into advances.

As a youngster, Thomas Edison was a candy vendor on the trains. One day, a man lifted Tom onto a train by his ears, and that ridiculous act caused his deafness. Throughout his life, Mr. Edison had a marginal ability to hear. But he did not curse it; he conquered it! I am sure if we had had a hypothetical interview with this phenomenal American at the peak of his career, it would have gone something like this:

"Mr. Edison, hasn't your deafness . . . ?"

"What's that?"

"Can't hear me?"

"Uh, er . . . ."

"OK — Mr. Edison, hasn't your deafness held you down? Hasn't it kept you back?"

"Listen, my friend," he replies, "to the contrary! Deafness has been a great help to me. For one thing, it has saved me from having to listen to a lot of worthless chatter. And it has taught me to hear from within."

LEAD YOUR MISFORTUNE!

I stood looking at a beautiful picture in the living room of a church member. The house was resplendent with lovely pictures, painted by the wife, but this particular winter scene showed the countryside heaving under glistening white snow. In the background was a charming farm house, with icicles dangling like diamond pine cones around the edge of the roof. The lake in the foreground was covered with a thick layer of ice — perfect for skaters on a winter afternoon. A boy and girl, tightly snuggled in each other's arms, skated into the mild sun reflecting shadows behind them.

"They're shadow-leaders," I said.

"Shadow-leaders?" queried my hosts.

"Yes! See, they're skating into the light. They're leading their shadows."

Some people follow their shadows — misfortunes. The past, with its flops, and faults, and falls, and scratches, and hurts, keeps in front of them, dooming them to defeat. Others walk into the light. They aren't afraid to be human, and their hopes aren't torpedoed. Looking ahead, they are triumphant shadow-leaders:

Today — with its misfortunes — is their opportunity to live. Tomorrow is their friend. They accept difficulty as a stepping-stone instead of a tombstone. They understand that life may be overwhelming or overcoming, and they are overcoming. They discover that no pressure need pressure them. They recognize challenges as men-makers, not men-breakers. Peaceful and quiet living is theirs. They are Discoverers!

Watch out for *pre-living!* It is a misfortune and it generates more of them. Living prior to the moment usually upsets you. One man told me that he pre-lived confrontations with his wife.

"I live out the situation beforehand. Often I get mad — hopping mad!"

His face looks like a person in actual argument. It flushes red. The eyes bug out in anger. The nose stiffens. He grits his teeth, and finds himself talking to himself — going through all the motions of a real verbal battle. The blood pressure shoots sky-high. This is a losing proposition.

Beware of *post-living!* It is living the fact over after the fact. This, too, is defeating, for it produces regret and guilt. One Sunday, I looked from the pulpit of my congregation and saw a worshiper whom I thought to be an old friend.

"No," I thought, "that can't be. He isn't in this part of the country."

I hadn't seen him in several years, but, sure enough, it was my friend. He had been in an upheaval, almost at the end of his rope. But, after seeing one of our telecasts, he boarded a plane late one evening, checked into a local hotel at six the next morning, and was in church by eleven. "I want to talk to you," he said after the worship service. I could see that he was a troubled man.

For the next two days, he poured out his predicament. Regret had set in after he had made the final decision to turn down the vice-presidency of a great insurance company. "The sorriest mistake of my life," he said. Within two weeks after that decision was made, the walls seemed to crash in on him. I asked if the doors were completely closed. He answered yes.

"Then, close it in your heart and go on to the door somewhere in front of you. There's another one out there. The Lord will help you find it, if you'll trust Him." A lot of his problem was wound up in post-living.

When you relive a setback, you may miss the opportunity of the moment! Keep your eyes ahead!

Start *peaceful living!* This is living with deep resources. The new Crocker-Citizens skyscraper in Los Angeles is a plush building. The office of a man whom I am proud to claim as a friend occupies the better part of the sixth floor. When I walked into his office one day, I noticed a beautiful plaque on his slick, mahogany desk. It had only one word on it: CHRIST.

"A conversation piece?" I asked.

"Yes, and more," Jack replied. "It's a constant reminder that Christ is the Source of Supply for everything I need, everything I am, everything I have, and everything I want to become." One of the most enthusiastic and successful businessmen on the West Coast has discovered the resources for turning misfortune into a fortune.

LIFE-LIFTER

A misfortune can be converted into His-fortune — a blessing from Christ to you!

NINTH DISCOVERY

A supply of amazing optimism

Usually, the troubled person is having a problem with his attitude. He is crossed up in his mind and foggy in his approach to life. Like the woman who told me she must have forty-five minutes and six cigarettes before she faces anyone in the morning, he is sluggish and short-fused. A problem looks like a mountain, because he thinks of it as that big.

Dr. J. A. Hadfield, the outstanding American counselor, once tested the strength of three men on his dynamometer. Each was instructed to grip the dynamometer and squeeze as tightly as he could.

Under normal conditions, their average grip was 101 pounds. Then the men were hypnotized and told they were weaklings. The average grip dropped to a ridiculous low — 29 pounds! Under hypnosis again, Dr. Hadfield told them they were strong — he-men. The average grip skyrocketed to 142 pounds — a 500 percent increase over their previous weak performance!

What was the difference?

Conditions and environment were the same; the men were the same. *The difference was what they held to be true!*

I know of a management specialist who takes over sick businesses and nurses them back to health. He says that over 90 percent of the problem is not in the business, but in the people who run it. The business will work out, when those in it work out. Consequently, he devotes much of his time pulling people up. It is very effective in getting to the heart of the difficulty, for, usually, their thoughts are restrictive. "Can't" fences them in. Life has become a "no." He gets them to affirm life.

What happens? Life and business become a wonderful "yes."

Another dramatic case is recruit Jess Fenton. Jess is a 64-inch, 135-pounder — a pint-size man. But he turned in the greatest physical effort ever recorded in Marine Corps history! "Fenton believes he's a 30-foot giant," remarked his sergeant. He *believes!* And that belief bears centrally on the thoughts!

In October of 1970, a battery of outstanding doctors, led by Professor Neil Miller, completed more than a decade of highly specialized research on the power of thoughts on the body. Their report, as announced in *Family Weekly* of January, 1971, shows that thoughts do really powerful things to your body. You can slow or increase the heart rate, lower the blood pressure, regulate the pulse, and even calm a spastic colon. Remember, they found this out in laboratory experiments with a large number of people involved!

Far from being a group of shallow, unqualified thinkers, these men scientifically reaffirmed what the Bible has taught for centuries.

Your thoughts build you or break you! Elevate your thinking! Get it up out of the pit!

Move ahead from second-class, energy-draining, life-whittling, enthusiasm-dwindling thoughts!

The quality of your life is in direct proportion to the quality of your thoughts.

Dr. O. A. Battista said that your thoughts can make you rich. They can also make you poor. If you swallow much of the stuff coming to you these days, you will soon be convinced that these are horrible, terrible, drastic times in which to live. They are challenging, yes! But when the power of optimism is in your heart, you are ready for them!

Pack your thoughts with good news! I, for one, am glad to hear that some television stations and newspapers have mounted a campaign for good news in this world. The *Wall Street Journal* announced that more newscasters and editors are emphasizing happy happenings. That's placing the emphasis on the right things. And they are getting amazing response from viewers and readers!

It has been proved that if you dwell on the bad, you will start spewing a bad tune. Think on the sour and you will turn sour; you will become a grouch.

It is like a record. Many of us have phonograph players and music. The favorite in our house seems to be the *Sound of Music*. Often our nine-year-old daughter, Darla, plays it morning and evening. It isn't hard to figure out what has happened. Unintentionally, she has memorized the songs. Now she sings merrily along with the Von Trapp family. And that joyful music creates a happy mood in her.

Thinking good news requires honesty — always — and truth, and right, as well as wholesomeness. There is

more than enough good news in life today with which
to fill your thoughts:

Over 200,000,000 Americans *will not* be arrested this
year!

Over 90,000,000 married Americans *will not* file for
divorce this year!

Over 115,000,000 Americans *will* maintain a formal
affiliation with some religious group this year!

Over 75,000,000 Americans and corporations *will* pay
more than $175 billion in income taxes this year!

Over 10,000,000 young Americans *will not* burn their
draft cards this year!

Over 4,000,000 teachers, preachers, and professors
will not strike or participate in riotous demonstrations this
year!

It all depends on whether one really wants to stress
the good or the bad; the positive or the negative; victory
or defeat. Someone told me that an optimist is one who
won't let his teen-age son drive the car and a cynic is
one who did! The solid optimist, however, is one who
sees the best.

"Opti" deals with sight. Derivatives include optical
and optician, which have to do with the eyes. "Mist"
is a root word for best.

A mark of the optimist is his feeling that the good of
life overbalances the pain and bad!

He looks for the best!

He applies the most favorable construction to events!

He anticipates a good outcome!

"We know that in everything God works for good with

those who love him, who are called according to his purpose" (Romans 8:28, RSV).

This Scripture is the roadmap for serious optimists — a sustaining motto for undefeatables! When it is reality, you become a happy-chondriac. You become hopeful.

Yes, you do have a choice. You may face life with fear, sneer, or cheer. When this optimism grips and shapes your spirit, you become a cheerful person. All the while, you are becoming a positive realist, even in the face of strenuous obstacles.

Do not mistake the optimist for a lackadaisical and careless Mr. Happy-go-lucky or Pollyanna. Nor is he a sour, grouchy Mr. Stern Face nor an unyielding Mr. Steel Will. Certainly he is not an up and down, in and out Mr. On-and-off. To him life gains depth! Life gets height. Life gathers width! Life becomes a creative and thrilling experience!

What is the outcome of this optimistic spirit?

OPTIMISM AFFECTS YOUR HEALTH

Dr. Robert Jackson, a physician of years ago, gave some rules for getting and keeping health: "Eat simple meals," he said, "and wear porous underwear." (That one can use some additional illumination!) I believe he reached the heart of the matter when he said, "Laugh often and become an optimist."

Dr. William Louden adds, "To insure good health . . . cultivate cheerfulness."

"Have a happy, loving frame of mind," advises Dr. Norman Beal. "It is mature health."

A Dr. Richardson claims that health is *not* merely a matter of the body. "Anger, hatred, and fear are among the influences most destructive of vitality."

What are these learned men saying? *Gloom and despair are just as likely to cause a disease as is a germ!*

Dr. Albert Hagedorn, head of the Department of Hematology and Internal Medicine at Mayo Clinic, feels that a depressed person suffers a slowing down of his metabolic processes. The doctor insists that some of their young patients die because they lack a cheerful spirit. Capitulating to hopelessness and gloom, they cave in like a helpless lamb before the big, bad bear.

A prominent physician told me that if he could be absolutely honest in his report to the coroner as to the cause of death for a thirty-six-year-old patient, he would write, "Gloomitis." "The man could be alive today," the doctor said. "He could be well on the way to recovery. But he was overcome by an attitude that he couldn't and wouldn't make it. Finally, he threw in the towel." "A merry heart doeth good like a medicine: but a broken spirit drieth the bones" (Proverbs 17:22, KJV).

Let's look at the opposite side of optimism—pessimism. Pessimism of your spirit weakens you physically to infectious attacks. It dampens the resistance of the body and tends to disorganize the physical formations. It may break down the discipline of cells and tissue. I know of no clearer example than Arnold Beall.

Barely past forty, Arnold is the president of a small electronics firm. The economic recession hit his company hard. Operating at a loss, he began to feel there was little hope of pulling out. This went on for a prolonged period of time—long enough for Arnold to start believing it. His blood pressure leaped sky-high. Colds, aches, and pains began to nag him.

"Funny," Arnold reminisced, "I knew that I had never been bothered by these things before." Formerly a specimen of fine health, in a matter of months he deteriorated to a "sickly infantile," as he described his dilemma.

(Contrast that with optimism. It strengthens you; pulls all forces together. Optimism unifies.)

One Monday, Arnold reflected on his problem. "There's something really wrong with me," he thought. "I've never been like this in the past. I've a hunch the trouble is inside." As if by accident, he read this verse from the Bible. (Arnold hadn't been reading it much lately, but he sensed a dire need to do so that particular day.) ". . . put on the new self [the new you] . . . the new man which God, its creator, is constantly renewing in his own image, to bring you to a full knowledge of himself" (Colossians 3:10, TEV).

"I couldn't get it out of my mind," Arnold said. "Put on the new self—the new man."

Tuesday morning was one of those beautiful California sunrises; the warm sunshine radiated through the glass of his car as he drove the freeway to his office.

"God," he prayed almost subconsciously, "I wish that sunshine would get into my heart."

"I am here, Arnold," he was assured, "and I touch *you.*"

"I believed it," he beamed, "and, Reverend, the most fantastic sensation swept over me! Honest to goodness, even the hair on my head tingled! A thrill raced down my body and twitched my toes! My finger tips came alive!

"The conflict melted away and I felt an indescribable release from tensions. The muscles in my face relaxed. A deep calmness came over me. I took an off-ramp and parked the car. I sat there, laughing and crying simultaneously. I knew that Christ was *here,*" he said, as he motioned to his heart.

Later that morning, his wife stopped by the office. "Arnie, dear," she said when she saw him, "what's happened?" He had a new glow and she could see it. Arnold's makeup — body as well as spirit — responded. The spirit behind genuine optimism had brought a new day to his life, and he knew it. Is it strange that he *is no longer* nagged by illnesses like a "sickly infantile"?

Arnold Beall is not alone in this discovery. Millions of upthinking, intelligent human beings of every age, race, and color have found that optimism affects one's health. And, through it, they have been aided to recovery.

OPTIMISM AFFECTS YOUR FEELINGS

It keeps you perky, and energetic, and enthusiastic. If you are feeling low, wilted, withered, beaten, and generally dried up, a dose of optimism will do wonders for you.

OPTIMISM AFFECTS YOUR APPEARANCE

Phillips Brooks, a great Christian of a few years ago, was always lively and radiant. Optimism makes people like that. On one occasion, a Boston newspaper spoke of Mr. Brooks in these terms: "It was a dull, rainy day, when things looked dark and lowering, but Phillips Brooks came down the street and all was bright." He didn't change the clouds, but his beaming spirit changed attitudes around him.

I've done a great deal of reading about many people, but one of the most optimistic men I have ever read about is Abraham. At one hundred years of age, while Sarah, his wife, was a youngish ninety, Abraham felt God leading them to have another child. The sacred record indicates that ". . . Abraham believed God even though such a promise just couldn't come to pass! And because his faith was strong, he didn't worry about the fact that he was far too old to be a father . . . and that Sarah . . . was also much too old. . . . Abraham never doubted. He believed God, for his faith and trust were strong, and he praised God for this blessing before it happened. He was completely sure that God was well able to do anything He promised" (Romans 4:18–21, LB).

What is the secret of the authentic optimist?

His trust is in the Lord. Thereby, he is attached, included, involved, yet free—ever so free! He is free in a deep freedom that really releases!

He believes that through everything that comes his way, he may realize a gain. God sees to it, and his God never lets him down.

He understands that the end of his own contriving may well be the beginning of God's arriving—so, he lets God.

He is certain there is a way out because there is a way up—always!

He can do the impossible because he sees the invisible. The impossible becomes a challenge.

To him, the outlook is as good as the "goods."

He exhibits this spirit through his life. Impression results in expression; imitation imparts illustration; registration leads to demonstration.

But where does the optimist start? He begins with an honest and open faith, which is the unbreakable backbone of optimism. "Believe God." No, it doesn't require a fullblown trust—only a heart sincerely open. You begin as a child.

Remember the mustard seed phenomenon? Jesus said that if you have faith as a grain of mustard seed — a tiny, but genuine faith — it is a definite beginning!

From there, you become more of an optimist, for your faith, like Abraham's, grows ever stronger until you reach a point of such confidence in God and oneness with the spirit of Christ that you thank God for blessings even before they happen. The amazing power of this optimism is seen in the life of Harv, a nineteen-year-old young man.

A short time ago, my phone rang in the early hours of the morning. "Reverend," quavered the man on the other end of the line, "my name is Harvey L. and I'm scared to death." He told me that he had watched our telecast and attended my church in San Dimas, California, several times, even though he lives an hour's drive away. I asked if he were drinking. "Oh, a martini or two," he answered, "but that's not my big hangup. I'm hopeless," he blurted out. He was in quite a predicament. For one thing, his fiancée was pregnant.

"Harv," I suggested, "now that you've called me for help, you'll have to follow the line I'm familiar with. Christ is the center of it. Are you willing?"

"That's what I called you for," he said.

"OK, let's pray."

I asked him to kneel beside his bed as I knelt beside mine. I talked to God for Harv and myself, then I invited him to pray.

"What shall I say?"

"Follow me," I advised, "and really mean it."

We prayed for help, confessed our wrongs, and thanked God for blessing us.

Harv began to sound like a different person. He talked more clearly, without strain or hesitation, as though his mouth was no longer dry, nor his tongue thick. I sensed that the Spirit of Christ was filling him and transforming him. That was the beginning.

The other day I received a letter from his mother. In it she listed four areas of improvement in Harv's life.

Desires He has a new world of wants, and it doesn't include what is harmful to him.

Enthusiasm about life He is excited about living. Now he gets up easily. Down in his heart, he feels that every day is the day the Lord has made.

Christianity He is finding out that it's fun to be a Christian. Christ is no long-faced, run-of-the-mill, out-of-step, irrelevant, willy-nilly washout!

Actions He has taken charge of the situation with his fiancée and they are working it out positively and sensibly. Would you believe he has her praying with him?

"For the first time in his life," Harv's mother wrote, "he is picking up his own socks and putting them in the laundry bag!"

From hopeless to hopeful — that's the tremendous power of optimism!

With this optimism, *your mind becomes a fertile field for deeper thoughts.* You discover a new receptivity to divine impulses. You may make the breakthrough on that tough problem you have been facing; gain the razor-sharp insight you have been needing; get the edge on things — an edge that has evaded you lately.

And you are a poised person.

POISE

A person is never on a high level when his thoughts are jittery. Jittery thoughts produce ruffled nerves, high blood pressure, and ragged relationships. They pull and tear. In fact, they are dangerous.

I shall never forget hearing the horrendous cries of a pilot who lost his poise. He wanted to land his plane, but below was a nasty storm. The controller in the tower advised the pilot that since he wasn't qualified to use the instruments in the aircraft, the tower would give him explicit directions. "Trust us completely," the controller bargained, "and we'll bring you home safely."

After the pilot was instructed to begin his descent, the tower heard screams of *"Help! Help! Help!"*

"Are you in a spin?" they radioed.

"Yes," shrieked the pilot in a high voice.

The controller gave explicit directions on what to do. "Acknowledge," he said. "Acknowledge."

There were a few tormented cries, but no intelligent reply. The pilot had panicked. In a few moments, radar contact was lost. He crashed, taking three lives with him.

Panic drives you to expediencies! Panic pushes you to extremes!

POISE BRINGS RATIONALE TO HOT TEMPERS. POISE SETTLES LIFE. POISE PREPARES THE WAY FOR YOU TO BE A CONTRIBUTION AT ALL TIMES. POISE WILL GET YOU MUCH FARTHER AHEAD.

A man whom I am proud to claim as a friend has a consistently calm spirit. He seems unsinkable. Even those closer to him than I am are startled at times. One day some workers in his office who didn't know him very well were discussing my friend.

"No doubt, he has a wonderful wife who helps him," one man conjectured.

"And," chimed in another, "his children aren't messed up with dope."

Someone else commented, "I bet they haven't had a sick day in their lives."

Still another, "Probably some rich uncle left him a fortune."

They thought these were the secrets to his poise.

Little did they realize that Mary, his wife, had just recovered from a rugged five-year fight with cancer; that he had spent much of his off-work hours caring for her. Little did they know that his oldest child was mentally retarded and his middle child had required many operations to correct nose and mouth deformities. Little did they understand that the youngest child had almost died of pneumonia years before and was still sickly. They didn't know that the income as a company accountant was the only source of funds the family had.

When there is a real optimism and it is used, you have a great calm-center at the core of all life. When life becomes a tempest in a teapot, you have what it takes to take it. The source within outthinks, outperforms, outbelieves, outstretches, and outlives the surroundings. There is fabulous peace!

You're a Discoverer!

LIFE-LIFTER

The Christian optimist is a realist who does something in life through the resources of his divine Friend. His supply never peters out!

Joy can be mine—always!

The longer I live, the more I feel that people may be genuinely happy, and this happiness can remain like a Rock of Gibraltar in the face of anything. (I assure you, I am talking about a heart-filled, need-deep joy, not phony, "ha-ha" stuff!)

I feel strongly that unhappy people are denying themselves, or are causing to be denied to themselves, the happiness they deserve.

But there is so much unhappiness. I see it among the churches. People come to worship, so sad the corners of their mouths drag on the ground.

A friend challenged the people in his congregation to watch the average person as he comes in. He shuffles along, pulling his lower lip behind him. He slides into his seat and hangs his glum face over the pew in front of him. He exudes the happiness of a skeleton and cross bones on a bottle of poison. (Probably his life is poisoned; and his life is poisonous!)

Someone claimed that the greatest football team in America would be ruined if the stadium was filled for four consecutive games with the average Sunday-morning congregation.

How long has it been since you really smiled? Since jolly laughter rolled out of your deep being? Stop for a moment, and turn toward a person nearby, and smile — now! "God bless" that person in your heart. You may be smiling at your wife, or husband, or child — and maybe it's the first time in years you've done it. They're surprised beyond words! But you feel better, too!

At the end of sixty minutes, more or less, worshipers leave the church to drivel through a dull week. Ministers aren't inexcusable either! I was told about two men at the clerk's counter in the hotel. As they waited, one asked the other, "Are you a minister?" and the other answered, "No, I just look like one, but I've had a prolonged sickness."

Some ministers seem to feel that if they can make worshipers feel gloomier and guiltier, they have accomplished their mission. I certainly refute that, for *God has given you a capacity for happiness and He intends for you to be filled.* "Always be full of joy in the Lord . . ." (Philippians 4:4, LB).

8 MORTAL ENEMIES OF PERSONAL HAPPINESS

A very impressive passage from the Bible outlines the enemies of personal happiness.

> Let everyone see that you are unselfish and considerate in all you do. Remember that the Lord is coming soon. Don't worry about anything; instead, pray about everything; tell God your needs and don't forget to thank him for his answers. If you do this you will experience God's peace . . . (Philippians 4:5-7, LB).

Selfishness

Selfish people are miserable human beings. These are the people who live to themselves only.

Joseph Newton succinctly pointed them out when he said, "When a man loses faith in God, he worships humanity; when faith in humanity fails, he worships science. . . . When faith in science fails, man worships himself, and at the altar of his own idolatry he receives a benediction of vanity. Hence," concluded Dr. Newton, "the tedious egotism of our day, when men are self-centered and self-obsessed, unable to get themselves off their hands."

They limp through life without life. Their spirit is like that of the father who prayed in the words of Walter Dudley Calvert:

> Lord, bless me and my wife,
> My son John and his wife,
> Us four and no more.

Or the childless couple who prayed

> Lord, bless us two,
> That will do. . . .

Or the bachelor who prayed

> Lord, bless only me,
> That's as far as I can see;

Or like the person who gave himself a party.

> I gave a little tea party
> This afternoon at three.
> 'Twas very small, three guests in all —
> I, myself, and me.

Myself ate up the sandwiches
While I drank all the tea,
'Twas also I who ate the pie
And passed the cake to me.
— AUTHOR UNKNOWN

They have themselves on their hands. Chances are they don't know what to do with what's on their hands. They can't stand themselves. If you are one of them, let peace bring happiness to you.

Inconsiderateness

Inconsiderate people are terribly unhappy. They snub the feelings of others. Roughshod, they run carelessly and needlessly over people, when there is another way to get to their objective; or there is an objective far superior to the one that will leave others dashed on the rocks of broken beings.

Loneliness

What about *lonely people?* They are miserable. A young woman who wrote to me is typical of this dilemma: "I have a big problem," she said. "Here I am, twenty-one years old, and I have never had a date. I have never been asked for a date. The best I can manage is a coke with friends — usually girls! I'm so lonely and my life is so empty."

I couldn't offer more than advice, but I know that if she finds a truly peaceful mental outlook and makes use of it in finding a man, it will work!

Worry

Worried people are unhappy. They squander energy on worry — energy they need to build happier lives. With a divided mind and a snarled life emptied of a tingling enthusiasm for each day, they siphon off happiness factors.

Prayerlessness

One of the biggest manufacturers of misery is *prayerlessness.* In a discussion with some brilliant, yet unbelieving young people, I maintained that a person's source must be deeper than oneself — higher than oneself. Authentic authority is *true self plus;* therefore, more than self. The person who is no deeper than himself is a shallow human being. And anyone who reaches no higher than himself doesn't have far to reach.

Prayer is utilization of the deeper and higher Source. Through prayer — honest, open, "God, I-am-yours" and "God, You-are-mine" prayer — your life sphere is stretched greatly.

The hymn writer expresses the idea.

> Oh, what peace we often forfeit,
> Oh, what needless pain we bear —
> All because we do not carry
> Everything to God in prayer.

Powerlessness

Another enemy of happiness is *powerlessness.* We live in a world that can be rough sometimes. Life is not always easy, nor should we expect it to be.

Four years ago, Bob jumped out of bed in the middle of the night. Judy, his wife, aroused enough to think, "Oh, he's going to get a drink of water." In a few moments, she heard a shattering sound. "Somebody's broken into the house and Bob's struggling with him," she thought.

Judy grabbed the phone and called the police, then she peeked into the living room and saw Bob sprawled out on the floor. There was no burglar — Bob had collapsed and, on the way down, he hit a coffee table.

Extensive examinations revealed nothing, so Bob went back to work. Life went on as usual for six months.

Then, while Bob was away on a business trip, he dropped unconscious in his hotel room. An associate traveling with him called a doctor. They flew Bob back home, ran another extensive series of tests, and discovered nothing. "Exhaustion," they concluded.

A year ago, it happened again. This time doctors discovered a tumor on his brain about the size of a golf ball. Surgery verified the soul-rending news that it was malignant. At thirty-four years of age, with three small children, my friend had to face the doctor's naked announcement: "We will do what we can."

"Yes," you may agree, "life can be tough." Often, most of us feel our problems are the world's worst! Whether or not they are, you need power, for powerlessness exposes you to unhappiness on all sides. But you may have power!

"Everything will be OK," Judy claimed, not without pain in her heart. I believe with her, for I have recounted these promises from Romans many times to this young housewife and mother: ". . . in everything God works for good with those who love him" (8:28, RSV). ". . . despite all this, overwhelming victory is ours through Christ Who loved us" (37, LB).

"I've prayed," she told me, "and I am doing all I know how to do. God will make things turn out, won't He?"

Yes!

Dr. Rollo May, the widely-known psychoanalyst, demands that *we find the center of strength to face and conquer the insecurities of this troubled age.* When you do, you will have power for happiness.

Thanklessness

Have you ever known a happy ingrate? Neither have I! I have discovered that gratefulness produces happiness and happiness brings on more gratitude.

If you will stop to think, you will give thanks — for then you will feel, deeply and honestly, about the many blessings you have. Be thankful for little blessings, big blessings, successes, and setbacks. Verbalize your gratefulness. Don't leave it hibernating in your thoughts. Make it known.

Peacelessness

The last mortal enemy of happiness is *peacelessness.* It is possible for you to be at peace within. Never allow anyone or anything to convince you otherwise. You must have peace within, or you will find life doubly difficult. Conflict is sure to confront you from the outside — that's life! But, when it is also hitting you from inside, you must fight on two fronts — and needlessly.

JOY SOURCES

A peaceful outlook offers hope because peace makes a person happy at the core of life. Discoverers are joyous people always — even when they are confronted with tough situations — because they have *joy-factors* in the *spirit* of their lives. Ten *joy-factors* are available to you.

Joy from What You Are Doing

John Dewey, the American educator, felt that the key to happiness is to find out what you are best suited to do and to secure the opportunity to do it. The Bible points out that each of us has the ability to do something well and we each have a different work to do (Romans 12:5), which is individual treatment.

French poet Jean Cocteau designed a stage set that required a tree as background. For weeks, he spent nights and days laboriously cutting out individual leaves for his tree. A friend, whose father owned a factory, suggested that they could manufacture the leaves mechanically. "Give me the design," he said, "and you'll have thousands of them before the week is over."

They mass-produced the leaves and pasted them on Cocteau's tree, but, when he stepped back to take a look at it, the poet commented that it was the most boring package of flat, uninteresting forms he had ever seen.

You are singularly-produced. God has not put you together on an assembly line, nor has He cut corners. You are unique and special—unrepeatable. You may not be beautiful; you may not like everything you see in your mirror—mental as well as physical—but you should sigh, "Thank God—I'm *me!*"

The point is: *You have the ability to do something which no one else can duplicate exactly.* Now, will you get about doing it? No more dilly-dallying; your life is too valuable!

Yes, you may and must enjoy yourself in your vocation. Dr. Charles Mayo had the idea: "There is no fun like work." A job is converted into a vocation by the pleasure it brings to you. You are exchanging time and talent for the product of what you are doing. Then, isn't it really important?

Joy from What You Are — Now!

You may change for the better! I hope you do.

But you need, also, to *enjoy yourself as you are.* No one is as good as he can be; and no one is as bad as he might be.

Self-condemnation is one of the most miserable producers of unhappiness you are up against. It will keep you pinned to defeat. Recognizing your mistakes and shortcomings, purposing to begin anew this moment in the confidence that each new second offers a fresh beginning, dwell on the good there is in you. This lends a positive excitement to the moment.

Joy from What You Are Becoming

Happiness never stops with what you are! A person may always become better, therefore, *you are a human being becoming.* What are you becoming? Sweet or sour? Believer or doubter? Winner or loser? Plus or minus?

You are becoming!

Ralph Waldo Emerson once said that the life of man is the true romance, which, when it is valiantly conducted, will yield a higher joy. That's becoming better.

Even modern science claims that there is happiness in becoming a better human being. It was brought out in one science symposium that joy is the effect that comes from using your powers. Joy is the emotion that accompanies the fulfilling of your nature as a human being.

"Keep putting into practice [day-by-day acts of becoming] . . . and the God of peace will be with you" (Philippians 4:9, LB).

Joy from Inner Completeness

When heart, mind, and body are pulling together, complete happiness doesn't depend on happenings. It rises from within. Joseph Addison points this out.

> True happiness is of a retired nature, and an enemy of pomp and noise; it arises, in the first place, from the enjoyment of one's self. . . . it loves shade and solitude . . . it feels everything it wants within itself, and receives no addition from multitudes of witnesses and spectators. On the contrary, false happiness loves to be in a crowd, and to draw the eyes of the world upon her. She does not receive satisfaction from the applauses which she gives herself, but from the admiration which she raises in others. She flourishes in courts and palaces, theatres and assemblies, and has no existence but when she is looked upon.
>
> — *The Spectator, No. 15, March 17, 1711.*

Are you complete enough to feel happiness from within? It doesn't take *things* to make you happy — rather, *you are* happy!

Joy from Stimulating and Worthwhile Goals

Goals represent you — what you are, what you think of yourself, what you do not think of yourself, what you feel you can become, and how valuable you consider your time to be.

The goals, or lack of goals, in your life reveal how big you believe God is — or how small! They reveal how much you believe God plus you can really accomplish, and how committed — or uncommitted — you are to doing it!

Establish objectives.

Pray for directions in setting them up.

Make them honest.

Be sure they are worthwhile.

Be sure they demand the highest and best of you.

One of the most unusual letters I have ever received came from a young couple who put a peaceful mental outlook into family goal-setting. In this letter, marked "Personal" and "Confidential," they requested that I officiate at the dedication of their beautiful baby girl.

Their letter reminded me that, in a sermon, I had challenged the congregation to "trust in the Lord and expect great results." They wanted a child desperately, so they decided to take me up on what I said — they asked God for a baby.

To really test it out, "taking the chance out of it," she explained, they prayed and believed for a conception in August. And, on the following May sixth, a precious girl was born into their family, making them deliriously happy. (Me, too!)

"The doctor verified the August conception," she added seriously.

That is a fantastic story — and sincere! It is unusual in terms of subject material, but illustrates clearly what true goals can contribute to one's personal happiness, especially when God is in them.

Joy from Nature

God's other creations — the mountains, lakes, streams, flowers, trees, and animal kingdom — contribute to our happiness. What can compare to the joy of a leisurely stroll through a pasture, a wood, or hills, serenaded by the swish of wind through the leaves? Listen to the trickle of water over pebbles; the soft melodies of birds; the flutter of a quail; the scampering of a squirrel; the bark of a dog; the moo of a cow; the cluck of a hen; the hee-haw of a donkey. Drink in the scent of the woods and the smell of newly plowed earth. Look into the rhythmic splendor of the sunset; the deep white of a cumulus cloud; the golden streaks across the sky at early sunrise.

You will burst out from the depth of your being, with a "Thank You! Thank You! Thank You, dear God!" And you feel the surging from within that the Psalmist felt when he adored: "The earth is the Lord's and the fulness thereof . . ." (24:1, KJV). "I will lift up mine eyes unto the hills from whence cometh my help" (131:1).

You experience a joy inside—a sensation unmatched by the impressive array paraded before humanity by modern science.

You feel an identification with God's creation, and you want to protect it. You want to help solve the environmental problems polluting our living space.

You become aware of the satisfaction supplied by God through His basic creation. Again, *things* lose their power in the face of magnificent simplicities. Ah, what joy there!

Joy from Strong Principles

The Webb School of California has 200 of the top high-school boys in America. For some time, the number of applications has far exceeded openings. Now, and since its inception, the school has matched high ideals and Christian principles with academic excellence, requiring the student body to put forth its best effort.

Dr. Thompson Webb shared with me the beginnings of his school. As a young man, he began on a shoestring, but he is a man of faith, so he believed it would work out. Seven days before the first semester, however, he had no students registered. Things looked dim, but during the next few days fourteen boys registered.

"I didn't know what sort of boys they were," he said. "It didn't matter anyhow. I needed warm bodies."

They turned out to be the rowdiest, most unprincipled fellows he had ever met. And they were uncontrollable. "I'll not stand for this," he told them and sent them home.

The Webb School had neither a student body nor a faculty three days after its grand opening. But people heard about his insistence on high ideals, work, and honest principles.

"Suddenly I had twenty-eight students!" he told me. Parents wanted their children in that positive environment.

"It didn't cost me anything except grief and failure to stand by my principles," said Dr. Webb.

A loose life produces a lean life! Unprincipled people are unhappy people. Perhaps you have tried to bring happiness out of itself, but happiness is not detached. It is not self-generated; it is attached — to strong, clean principles. Philip Skelton, the old Irish minister spoke wisely: "Our principles are the springs of our actions; our actions, the spring of our happiness or misery.

But principles are stale unless they result in wholesome living. Imagine developing a cure for cancer without using it! A principle, however worthwhile, has the effect of no principle, until it is implemented in constructive action. Alfred Adler, the gifted psychiatrist, felt that it is easier to fight for one's principles than to live up to them.

Living principles is a *joy-factor,* and a very positive one.

Joy from a Dynamic Fellowship

"Creative Fellowship" is a term for what the church needs to become again—and may become. In its revitalized life, the church is an invigorated group of creative believers who keep on getting more creative.

The fellowship is tied with the spiritual bond of faith; the spiritual is real through care, growing, sharing, united efforts, outreach, and *joy*. Faith always sparks a visible witness. "Don't hide your light! Let it shine for all . . ." (Matthew 5:15, LB).

The people are netted meaningfully in membership as an expression of this faith.

In my judgment, this represents the workings of a *Creative Fellowship*. But churchianity has crept onto the scene. Systems, institutions, machinery—these have almost swallowed up the honest mission and nature of the church. People became members of the system, supporters of the institutions, and names-on-the-roll only. If there were an alive experience of faith flowing out of the soul, it was skimpy. The church became a convenience-factor: used at birth, marriage, and the funeral, maybe for an Easter and Christmas excursion.

Now, churchianity is in a nose dive. Tremendous! I'm thankful! *Creative Fellowship* will not only survive—it will become stronger than ever! It *is* getting stronger! For *Creative Fellowship* has a key marking—life!

At every opportunity, I urge people to unite with my congregation—a *Creative Fellowship*. One person said, "Well, I know why you asked to see me. You want me to join your church sooner than I planned."

"Basically, you've arrived at the wrong conclusion,"

I answered. He appeared somewhat surprised when I assured him that I wanted to help him become a happier person. "That's the reason I asked you to come by."

He had a victorious glow on his face as he began to understand that the *Creative Fellowship* actually contributes to his personal joy and that of his family. You may glow, too, with this joy.

Tie into a *Creative Fellowship*. No, I am not suggesting that you leave your church. If your church is less than a *Creative Fellowship*, dedicate yourself to helping it become one—now! Start now! You're the one! You can do it!

Joy from Following Through

Essentially, people are "follow-throughs" or "fall-throughs."

"Fall-throughs" are unhappy individuals. Their intentions may be of high quality but, when it comes to carrying them out, they fall through. They may have grand ideas, powerful plans, and possibilities unlimited, but they fall through because people fail to consummate them in reality.

Follow through!

"Be sure to use the abilities God gave you. . . . Put these abilities to work; throw yourself into your tasks . . ." (I Timothy 4:14–15, LB).

Follow through on:

THOSE DESIRES FOR A HAPPIER MARRIAGE!

THAT PROJECT YOU'VE LONG DREAMED ABOUT!

GETTING THE CREATIVE FELLOWSHIP UNDERWAY!

GIVING LIFE YOUR BEST!

GIVING CHRIST YOUR ALL!

LAUGHING AT YOUR SILLY MISTAKES!

FORGETTING YOUR REGRETS!

CONTRIBUTING!

Joy from God

What other source of such reliability and capability is there?

A teen-ager understood this. After I conducted a memorial service for a well-known, well-loved man, I was standing close by, as attendants prepared to go to the grave site, when I noticed a slip of paper pinned on to the suit of the deceased man. I walked over to see what it was. This is what the note read: "Happiness is to be with God. I love you, Gramps."

How touching — how true!

But you need not wait for death to be with God. You can be with Him today and still be alive on this earth! You will really be alive, for life will flow throughout your whole system!

God can be with you today.

He truly wants this. My friend, Dr. E. Stanley Jones, said it this way in *The Way to Power and Poise:* "God couldn't be what He is if He didn't want to be where we are, in spite of what we are. He wants to live in us so that we may live in Him. He comes to where we are that we may be where He is."

By being with you, *in* you, God fills your life with peace. Joy is no longer a dream or a wish. It is experience! You become a spiritual millionaire. "Do you want to be truly rich? You already are if you are happy and good" (I Timothy 6:6, LB).

LIFE-LIFTER

Meet mankind's really great Joy-Giver: Jesus Christ! Commitment to Him of your life, as you are, starts you in joyous motion. Conscious commitment of each day, day by day, keeps the joy-tide up. Even when you are low, the low has a joyous meaning to it.